VIETNAM FOLLIES

A Memoir of an Intelligence Officer

By

Henry Billings

© 2002 by Henry Billings. All rights reserved.

No part of this book may be reproduced, stored in a retrieval system, or transmitted by any means, electronic, mechanical, photocopying, recording, or otherwise, without written permission from the author.

ISBN: 0-7596-7362-4

This book is printed on acid free paper.

1stBooks - rev. 12/10/01

ACKNOWLEDGEMENT

My deepest thanks to my wife, Melissa, whose thoughtful suggestions, encouragement, and editing made this book much better than it otherwise would have been.

Foreword

Since I left Vietnam in 1966, I have read many books on the war. I believe this book is unlike any of them. It is the story of my years as a conflicted young man who was opposed to the war but who felt a duty to serve his country. Luckily—and it was blind luck—I avoided the actual fighting. So this book is not about combat like half the books on the Vietnam War. And it is not written by a famous journalist like the other half of the Vietnam books out there. Instead, it is about an outsider stirring up trouble inside Army intelligence. What separates my effort from other books I've read is that I hated the Vietnam War and the Army *all along*. The question of fight or flight was always with me. Also, my job gave me unique insights into the numbers game played by the Army, especially with regards to B-52 attacks, enemy morale, and Cambodia.

CONTENTS

Chapter 1 ~ Student Soldier 1
Chapter 2 ~ You're in the Army Now.................................... 11
Chapter 3 ~ Welcome to Saigon 24
Chapter 4 ~ Settling In 43
Chapter 5 ~ Garbage In—Garbage Out................................... 57
Chapter 6 ~ Mean Streets 73
Chapter 7 ~ Murder—Saigon Style... 83
Chapter 8 ~ The Mouse That Roared 92
Chapter 9 ~ The Reds and the Blues 106
Chapter 10 ~ Down Time... 117
Chapter 11 ~ The Loving Cup 126
Chapter 12 ~ Taking Leave 134
Chapter 13 ~ Going Back... 142

VIETNAM FOLLIES
A Memoir of an Intelligence Officer

Chapter 1 ~~ Student Soldier

Naturally the common people don't want war… Voice or no voice, the people can always be brought to the bidding of the leaders… All you have to do is tell them they are being attacked and denounce the pacifists for lack of patriotism.
—Herman Goering

I was a bad soldier. I wasn't really bad in the way many bad soldiers are bad. I knew how to follow orders, shine my combat boots, and line up the buttons on my shirt with my belt buckle. Marching in step to the drumbeat wasn't a problem, nor did I have trouble understanding how to turn in the right direction. I could sing songs with lyrics that rhymed with various parts of the female body. I even figured out how to take apart and put together again an M-1 rifle with my eyes closed. So—on the surface at least—I looked like the All-American boy in uniform.

But I had one problem. I was a bit of a pacifist. I wasn't a doctrinaire like a Quaker or Mennonite. If pressed, I knew I would stand my ground and fight. Growing up as a Boston Braves fan in a Red Sox town, I'd had plenty of practice doing that. But I had trouble with the concept of killing total strangers just because the United States said to do it. Killing in general bothered me. I loathed capital punishment and condemned those who hunted Bambi for sport.

So from the army's point of view, I wasn't the most promising material. Still, I gave it a shot. It seems quaint now, but at the time I honestly felt that I had a duty to my country. I owed Uncle Sam two years of my life. In the early 1960's, that was a belief shared by just about every other American boy on the verge of manhood. My parents shared this belief.

Henry Billings

My father actually thought I should consider making a career out of the army. He had a sixth grade education and worked all his life in the building trades as a plasterer and a pipe coverer. Dad went from one construction job to another with periods of unemployment in between. He hated being without work. So when he wasn't working, he was looking for work. He never took a real vacation until he finally retired at the age of 72. He didn't want that for his sons. For him, the main goal in life was to find a steady job. In junior high school I signed up for the college track which included Latin and all the hard sciences. Dad thought I was nuts. "What kind of a job will Latin get you?" he asked. If he'd had his way, I would have taken nothing but shop classes and what he called elocution lessons. If I learned to speak well enough, Dad reasoned, I might become a union leader some day. Union leaders had steady work. He never encouraged me to be a lawyer or a doctor. That was beyond his vision. But he could see me as a union boss. That was within his frame of reference.

My mother had an eighth grade education and worked cleaning toilets at Harvard University to help me through college. I never once heard my father or mother talk about politics or political leaders. Both were go-along-to-get-along types so I never discussed my changing political views with them.

*****

Still, I was their son and had some of their Boy Scout values. So I reasoned that if I had to serve in the military, I would rather be a second lieutenant than a private. (If I had known at the time that a higher percentage of second lieutenants die in combat than any other rank, I might have given it more thought.) So, in 1960, I joined army ROTC as an undergraduate, first at Northeastern University and—after transferring—at the University of Massachusetts. There was a monetary angle to my decision, too.

VIETNAM FOLLIES
A Memoir of an Intelligence Officer

I needed the $29 a month the government paid me. It wasn't much. But this was a time when tuition was $100 a semester and Happy Hour draft beers cost a dime.

So there I was—on the one hand a Boy Scout and on the other hand a bleeding-heart leftist. These internal personalities didn't make the best soul mates. I could never take army drills seriously. I had no close friends in ROTC. Most of my best friends were fellow leftists who didn't buy my argument that I owed something to my country.

Of course, I didn't spend all my time in ROTC. For some long forgotten reason, I majored in business. (It was a poor choice. As my life unfolded, I never once managed any business larger than that of a freelance writer.) U Mass business classes at that time lacked rigor. In fact, they had such a soft reputation that Draper Hall—where the classes were taught—was known as Draper High.

Beyond the courses I had to take for my major, I squeezed in all the history and political science classes I could. Most of the time, I was in ROTC denial. No one else in ROTC was also a card-carrying member of the United World Federalists and the International Club. No other cadet campaigned for Harvard Professor H. Stuart Hughes, the "peace" candidate and advocate of nuclear disarmament in the 1962 Massachusetts Senate race won by Edward Kennedy. No one else in ROTC read leftist journals such as the *Minority of One* and *Ramparts*. It wasn't easy being a One-World advocate while learning to kill a man from behind without letting him make a peep.

Slowly, the leftist side of my brain began winning most of its battles with the rightist side. By 1963—in the middle of my junior year—I hated the army. I really, really hated it. But it was too late. I didn't have the nerve to quit. I certainly didn't want to become eligible for the regular army draft again; that would be a one-way ticket into the infantry and cannon-fodderhood. And fleeing the country at this point didn't cross my mind. (In 1963, Vietnam was just a minor irritant to most Americans, a minor bush war with no regular army units involved. The most likely flash point still seemed to be Berlin. If I was going to get my ass shot off, I continued to assume it would happen in Europe.) So I muddled along, living two lives. The leftist-pinko may have won most of the battles, but when push came to shove, the Boy Scout won the war. I stayed in ROTC.

*****

In the summer of 1963, I spent six weeks at Fort Devens in Massachusetts. This was not optional. Every ROTC cadet had to go to summer camp after his junior year. It was army boot camp, although technically we were still college students and not in the army. We hadn't yet been commissioned as second lieutenants. So we did all the things that privates have to do in the real army—peel potatoes, mop floors, clean toilets, sleep in barracks, make beds so that a dropped quarter will bounce halfway to the ceiling. We also learned to sleep head to toe. This, the army told us, was to protect against airborne disease spread by—what?—bad breath? I could never figure it out. And I found it impossible get a good night's sleep with the smelly toes of two other men sticking in my face.

If the nights were bad, the days weren't much better. We spent most of the time playing war games in the rolling woods and fields of Fort Devens. This was not my strong suit. I was a city boy who grew up thinking the Boston Commons was the country. Any squad or platoon I led into mock battle was quickly either captured or annihilated. But there was no harm done. At night, over a few beers, I could all laugh at my blunders. And running around in the woods was kind of fun.

For me, the real problem came with the army's attempts at psychological indoctrination. The most striking example of this was bayonet training. I knew the odds of actually getting into hand-to-hand combat were damn slim. In 1963, U Mass had an armor program. That meant all of its graduates would ride into combat in a tank, like George Patton. Still, the army figured that a little bayonet training could help put its recruits in the mood to kill. So one hot day in July we filed into some bleachers to learn the fine art of thrusting a bayonet into a man's stomach and lifting up. Our instructors showed us how to unsheathe the bayonet, fasten it to the end of an M-1, and charge at the straw dummies. The trick was to put our heart and soul into the charge. We had to scream, "Kill! Kill! Kill!" as we raced towards the target. We were told to stick the bayonet in hard—really hard. Then we were to pull it out at the same angle it went in. Otherwise the blade might get stuck on the man's rib cage. We were supposed to be quick and lethal. It might be a long day with lots of other fathers, brothers and sons to kill.

Soon all the cadets were jumping up and down on the bleachers, screaming, "Kill! Kill! Kill!" You had to be there to believe it. All these bright-faced history and English literature majors crying for blood. I couldn't do it. So I stood silently on the top row of the bleachers. That was a mistake. One of the drill instructors noticed my lack of enthusiasm. He raised his hand to silence the other cadets. Then he pointed his finger at me and said, "Get down here."

Since there was no place to hide and I couldn't very well leap off the back of the bleachers and run away, I made my way down through the other cadets. They parted like the Red Sea. For them, this had to be a delicious moment. Most knew how I felt about the military. Now they were going to get a free sideshow, a circus act. The drill instructor didn't disappoint them. He ordered me to jump up and down and scream, "Kill! Kill! Kill!" He was in my face for five minutes before I did it loud enough to inflate the veins in my neck. He was on me the rest of the day, telling me to "get with the program." "Stick him harder, soldier!" "Thrust and lift, you pussy!" "For Christ sakes, give me that rifle!" He jammed the blade in so hard I thought he was going to rip the dummy off its stays. "There! Now he's dead!"

Henry Billings

Somehow I got through the six weeks. In fact, I must have graded out fairly high in most other subjects. When I returned for my senior year at U Mass, they made me a cadet lieutenant colonel. There was one senior cadet colonel and a couple of cadet lieutenant colonels. The rest of the seniors were either majors or captains. Among the cadets, then, I was the second highest-ranking officer. It wouldn't be the first time the army's judgment of me was deeply flawed. But there I was, almost at the top of the power structure. It wouldn't last long.

Quickly, the bloom came off the rose. In the fall of 1963, we were practicing close-order drill. Most of the time we did this in civilian clothes. ROTC classes were scheduled just like all other classes on campus. We met at, say, 10 AM every Monday, Wednesday, and Friday. So ROTC class came directly on the heels of some other class. We didn't have time to change into a uniform. We came as we were.

But here the army had its own rules. Civilians clothes or not, they considered us to be in "uniform" even if it consisted of nothing more than jeans and a T-shirt. Well, this day I had pinned a "Vote Socialist" button on my shirt. When my instructor saw the button, he went wild. He told me I was a disgrace to the uniform and the army. There was no place for a pinko in his class, he said. With the Constitutional right of free expression clearly on my side, he eventually cooled off—but not before he assigned me a 50-page research paper on the history of the Sherman tank. When word of the punishment spread through the ranks, a hero appeared. His name was Captain Charles Huggins. He was my personal ROTC advisor. Captain Huggins took pity on me. He apparently talked to the drill instructor and had the punishment removed. Two years later, Captain Huggins was in Vietnam as an advisor to a South Vietnamese army unit. His picture made the cover of *Newsweek*.

Still, the campaign button was not forgotten. The PMS (Professor of Military Science), a regular army colonel whose name I've forgotten, asked me to report in uniform to his office.

VIETNAM FOLLIES
A Memoir of an Intelligence Officer

The Colonel was head of the entire corps. He was not someone to mess with. But – (and these days I shake my head, wondering what the hell I was thinking)—I decided to mess with him anyway.

The Colonel looked me in the eye and asked, "Son, are you proud of your uniform?"

This, of course, was one of those questions that has only one answer. But in a moment of madness, I tried the other alternative. "No, sir." I didn't say it to make him angry. I was already in enough trouble. And I knew Captain Huggins had gone to bat for me. So I didn't want to appear to be a total jerk. But the words just tumbled out of my mouth as if they had been putting their collective shoulders to the back of my teeth since breakfast. Once out, I had to make a plausible defense of my position. The angry and blue-faced PMS demanded to know what I meant. I did the best I could to defend the indefensible. Yes, I said, I was proud of the uniform worn by the soldiers in the Revolution. They fought for freedom and independence. And, yes, I was also proud of the World War II uniform which defeated Hitler and Tojo. On the other hand, I wasn't proud of the uniform that wiped out the American Indian. I wasn't proud of the uniform that stole the American Southwest from the Mexicans. And I wasn't particularly proud of the uniform that turned the Philippines into a colony. On balance, I continued—I was fudging a bit now—the issue of pride was a toss-up. Good wars, yes. Bad wars, no.

To the Colonel's credit, he didn't pull out a .45 from his drawer and shoot me dead on the spot. He did, however, demote me. He stuck out his hand and asked for one of my two diamonds from each shoulder. (Two diamonds signified a cadet lieutenant colonel.) Now I had one diamond on each shoulder. That meant I was only a cadet major. I reveled in this briar patch punishment. It reduced my duties and made me a less conspicuous figure. By then I had lost whatever friends I had in ROTC. That was all right. Even then, U Mass was a big campus.

Henry Billings

Yet when I think back to that and other such incidents from my current perspective as a middle-aged man awash in easy-going moderation, I can't help but shudder.

Just before I graduated in 1964, the army announced a change in policy. U Mass was no longer an armor school. ROTC graduates could pick any branch of the army they wanted so long as there was an opening. Most of the graduates picked one of the three combat branches—armor, artillery, or infantry. In a heartbeat, I chose intelligence. Imagine, me as *I*. Maybe I would be a spy or something. In any event, I probably wouldn't have to kill anyone and intelligence promised to be more interesting than, say, quartermaster or the signal corps. In one of life's lucky breaks, the army needed intelligence officers and I got in. Even so, I was in no rush to join the army. I had up to a year to report for active duty, so I took my sweet time. I spent the fall of 1964 hitchhiking and backpacking through Europe. (When I hitchhiked, I hung a small American flag from my right wrist. I figured it would improve my chances of getting a ride. On the whole, it did. Most Europeans at the time still liked Americans. Five years later, at the height of the Vietnam War, anyone donning a U.S. flag other than on the seat of their pants was asking for trouble.) I grew up in Somerville, Massachusetts and had never been farther away from home than California. I wanted to see more. I was happy just walking down the road with my thumb out. If no one gave me a ride for hours, that was OK. I was free to do whatever I liked and had all the bread and cheese I could eat.

Meanwhile, news from the other side of the world was growing worse. The assassination of South Vietnam's leader Ngo Dinh Diem on November 1, 1963, encouraged by a wink and a nod from the United States, had solved nothing. The generals who followed Diem were either incompetent or corrupt. So, by the summer of 1964, the United States was looking for any excuse to take over the war effort. Up to that point, the 15,000 or so Americans soldiers in Vietnam had served only as advisors. As yet, there had been no American combat units in Vietnam. On August 2 of that year, a North Vietnamese patrol boat "attacked" the *U. S. S. Maddox* in the Gulf of Tonkin. It suffered one bullet hole one inch in diameter. Two nights later, the *U. S. S. C. Turner Joy* reported that torpedoes had been fired at it from North Vietnam. No proof was ever found of an assault.

Nonetheless, three days later, the United States Congress overwhelming passed the Gulf of Tonkin Resolution, giving President Lyndon Johnson virtually unlimited war powers. (There were two "no" votes in the Senate. These were cast by Wayne Morse of Oregon and Ernest Gruening of Alaska. In the House, there were no hearings and only one hour of debate. House members had war fever. The resolution passed unanimously.)

Soon U.S. planes launched their first air strikes against North Vietnam. Then, in October, Communist China exploded its first atomic bomb. Asia was getting more and more interesting with each passing day. But as yet, I couldn't see the writing on the wall in terms of my future. No one was talking openly about sending combat troops to Vietnam.

In Europe, just about all the young people I met at youth hostels and on the road believed the United States had no right to be in Vietnam at all. The French were especially hostile. While I generally shared their sentiment, I found French criticism of the United States hard to take, given their own dismal track record in Indochina. Some Europeans even took shots at Kennedy's Peace Corps. It was, they said, old imperialism in new bottles. I grew slightly defensive. The Boy Scout in me rose to justify America's foreign policy. But I don't think I convinced anyone. It's hard to win many arguments when you don't believe your own side.

The presidential election of 1964 loomed large in my view. Before I left the States, I cast an absentee ballot for Lyndon B. Johnson. (I had also written a letter to the editor that was published in *The New York Times* attacking Barry Goldwater's acceptance speech at the Republican convention.) I felt that once Johnson was elected president in his own right, things would get better. Surely Johnson would temper the Cold War zealots left over from the Kennedy Administration who were still itching "to pay any price, bear any burden, meet any hardship, support any friend, oppose any foe to assure the survival and success of liberty.".

Johnson was, in my view, the "peace" candidate. Goldwater had hinted that maybe a nuke or two would shorten the war in Vietnam. If Goldwater had won the election, I don't know what I would have done. I thought seriously of just staying in Europe. If the Army wanted me, it would have to come and get me. Fortunately, I never had to face that choice. Johnson won in a landslide, so I thought it was safe to return home. Still, in terms of anti-war sentiment, I was ahead of the curve. My head in 1964 was in a place that most people didn't reach until after the Tet Offensive in 1968.

I arrived back in the States in November and went straight to Mount Snow in southern Vermont to spend some time as a ski bum. I got a job working in the kitchen of a ski lodge. The place had once been owned by Teddy Roosevelt and later used, on occasion, by Lowell Thomas for his radio broadcasts. The work was easy and there was plenty of time to ski and party. I wanted to make the most of it. Time was running short. As heavyweight champ Joe Louis once said about a fleet-footed foe, "You can run but you can't hide." I had been running away for nearly a year. But there was no hiding from the Army. I had a two-year obligation. All I wanted was to get in, do my time, and get out.

VIETNAM FOLLIES
A Memoir of an Intelligence Officer

Chapter 2 ~~ You're in the Army Now

I wanna be an Airborne Ranger,
I wanna live a life of danger,
I wanna die in the old drop zone,
Box me up and ship me home.

I wanna be an Airborne Ranger,
Live the life of sex and danger,
I wanna go to Vietnam,
Kill some commies for my mom.
      —Army marching song

On April 30, 1965, I reported for active duty at Fort Benning in Georgia. The first order of business was to survive two months of infantry training. The army called it IOBC, or Infantry Officer's Basic Course. Every 2nd lieutenant coming out of ROTC had to get through IOBC, regardless of whether he was in signal corps, infantry, intelligence, or any other branch of the army.

The Benning program was a lot tougher than summer camp at Fort Devens. I wasn't a college student any more. I swore a real oath and was in the real army. Although all of us had our army commissions, anyone who washed out of IOBC would lose it. That was the sword the army held over my neck. Screw up here and I would not only lose my commission, I would go to the top of the draft list. Enough said. I definitely did not want to flunk IOBC. But how was I going to ensure that didn't happen?

For the first few weeks I marched, took classes, and did physical training. That part was fairly easy. I scored well on the paper and pencil tests and by the end of the third week ranked near the top of the class of 140 officers. To pass IOBC, I had to accumulate a certain number of points. I don't remember the exact amount but it was something like 200. If you were perfect in everything, you could score maybe 300 points. But, again, you needed at least 200 to keep your commission. My goal was to break out of the gate fast and build up a long early lead; I would need as much of a cushion as I could get before we turned to the real infantry stuff.

Eventually the focus shifted to the firing range, hand-to-hand combat, bayonet training, and war games. The bayonet training was much more realistic than it had been at Devens. We found ourselves crawling under barbed wire with real explosions kicking up chucks of red mud and live fire whistling over our heads. Crawling never had been my long suit. At 6 feet, 3 inches, my ass always stuck up in the air. Luckily, the soldier manning the machine guns aimed high and didn't shoot it off.

While I was at Benning, rumors began to fly that a few of us might go to Vietnam. Back in March, the U. S. Marines had landed two battalions to defend the airfields in Danang. They were the first U.S. combat units to enter Vietnam. By July, there were eighteen combat battalions in country and more in the pipeline. That sucking sound we heard was conventional wisdom flushing down the drain. Despite the warning of many wise men – men such as Dwight Eisenhower—we were now getting involved in an Asian land war. And despite John F. Kennedy's claim that it was "their war," it was rapidly becoming "our war." The United States was doing just what we'd said we wouldn't do. We were sending American boys to take the place of Asian boys on the front lines.

Still, to those of us training at Fort Benning that summer, the rumors were just that: rumors. Most of us continued to think that we would be sent to Germany or some stateside post. As the weeks passed, my rank in the class headed due south fast. But my plan had worked to perfection. I had collected more than 200 points, enough to ensure my graduation. That was a good thing because the grand finale of all our training was something called Escape and Evasion. It was run by the army Rangers and was

VIETNAM FOLLIES
A Memoir of an Intelligence Officer

their version of a final exam. This exercise was worth 30 points. It was a pass/fail test; a trainee either got 30 points or he got nothing. A few of my fellow officers desperately needed those 30 points to retain their commission, so for them this was serious business. For me, though, the exercise was just another reminder that I was now a soldier. I wanted to skip it altogether, but there was no chance of that. Points or no points, the army insisted that all trainees participate.

I had dreaded Escape and Evasion from the first time I heard about it—and with good reason. The object of the exercise was simple. Each man had to infiltrate through "enemy" lines and reach a designated point. If you were captured along the way, you were held as a prisoner. The test was set up so that only a few of us would make it. The rest would be captured and experience, briefly, life as a POW. The real goal of the Escape and Evasion was to give us a taste of enemy interrogation. (We were taught to give only our name, rank, and serial number.) A bit of torture was to be expected. The Rangers told us about some of the possibilities and our imagination did the rest. I particularly remember the technique they called "sitting on the pole." The Rangers tied you to a pole in such a way that the back of your legs supported the entire weight of your body. You might stay that way for hours. (Clearly, it was not a good idea to get caught early in the exercise.) Even the toughest man, we were told, could be reduced to tears tied to that pole. Escape and Evasion was a night exercise. Before it began, the Rangers gave us a briefing. Basically, this consisted of them saying they were really going to "get" us.

Time for a little history. There had been some trouble in an IOBC class earlier in the spring. The story we heard was that the Rangers had captured one of the trainees, tied his hands behind his back and dumped him out of the back of a truck. The fall broke his back. One of the men in that IOBC class was a Harvard graduate and very well connected. As I recall, his father was the American ambassador to Switzerland. Anyway, the Harvard guy called his dad and told him what had happened. The ambassador called Washington to complain. That led to an army investigation. The next IOBC class was very closely monitored by the Inspector General, so the Rangers had to keep the exercise within reasonable limits. No one was killed or maimed.

Now, however, the inspectors were gone. It was just my luck to be in the first IOBC to come along since they had left. The Rangers were itching to resume their old ways. They didn't hide their intentions, either. They delighted in scaring the shit out of us with all their talk of the tortures they had planned. I think they meant it in part as a challenge. It was red meat stuff. But I was ordering vegetarian. I wanted nothing to do with playing the game or scoring the 30 points.

Thinking back on it now, I'm amazed by what a powerful death wish I had. There is just no other way I can explain my actions that afternoon. At the time, however, I told myself I simply wanted to have a little fun. (All right, I admit it: I was also secretly also hoping the army would find me "temperamentally unfit for military duty.") In any case, 139 trainees prepared for the Escape and Evasion by dressing up in full infiltration garb. They blackened their faces, taped over belt buckles, wore black caps pulled tight over their heads and so forth. I did none of this. Instead, I washed my face to a bright sheen, left my canteen dangling loose, and put on a white tennis flop hat with a "Ranger" badge glued across the front.

In the early evening, the entire class formed up in front of our barracks. I, of course, stood out like a snowball against a pile of coal. The Rangers could not believe their eyes. "Who the fuck is this guy?" I could hear them muttering. Then they got in my face. They screamed up and down and called me every name in the book. They threatened me. They even put a bounty on my head. They announced that whoever captured me would get a case of cold beer and a three-day pass.

Privately, the Rangers really were scaring the shit out of me. But I would be damned if I was going to let them know that.

VIETNAM FOLLIES
A Memoir of an Intelligence Officer

"You haven't got me yet," was all I said. At the appointed time, all the trainees piled into trucks and were driven to the drop-off point. When we got there, we jumped out and stood together along the road. There really was no "escape" unless you count getting out of the truck. The true task was evasion. The thick Georgia woods in front of us was filled with "enemy" soldiers. Our job was to somehow "evade" them. It wouldn't be easy. The enemy had laced the woods with all sorts of trip flares. One false step and the ground around you would light up like a Christmas tree. The enemy soldiers sat in the woods grinning. They knew the odds were heavily stacked in their favor.

As soon as it got dark enough, the signal was given. The trainees spread out along the road. Then all of them slowly crept north into the woods. All except one. I headed south. There was absolutely no way I was going to enter those woods and get captured. So I snuck off into the woods on the wrong side of the road and soon found a small hill with an excellent view of my fellow trainees. I covered myself with leaves and waited. It wasn't long before flares lit up the sky. Screams and shouts followed. Most of the trainees were captured within a few hours. Others made it through the first line of enemy soldiers only to be captured later.

Fewer than 10 trainees actually got to the designated spot and won the 30 points. My roommate. Ed Dandar, was one. He was one of the trainees who needed the points to hang onto his commission. To get those points, however, Ed had to wade through a swamp outside the boundary of the woods. The Rangers had told us that the swamp was off-limits. The reason they gave was that the area was filled with poisonous snakes. Personally, I thought it was because none of the Rangers wanted to spend the night in that cold, wet swamp waiting for us to fall into their arms. In any case, although he broke that rule, the Rangers lauded Ed for his initiative and courage. Good soldiers, they told him, don't always follow the rules. (When Ed Dandar got to Vietnam, he requested a transfer to a combat unit in the delta south of Saigon. Happily, he made it through his tour alive.)

Meanwhile, back on my hill, I had dozed off. Sometime after midnight I awoke, walked down the hill, crossed the road, and entered the woods. I figured that by this time everyone had moved to the far end of the woods. Certainly all the enemy soldiers would be gone from this part of the woods. They would be off chasing the few trainees who were still on the loose. So I felt fairly safe. As I made my way through the woods, I came across two other trainees who had been hiding near the starting line. They, too, had waited until it seemed safe to move. Because they had stayed within the official boundaries of the exercise, they had been much closer to the action. They had actually seen some of the other trainees get captured. They agreed with me that not playing the game by the rules had been a brilliant choice.

The Escape and Evasion exercise was scheduled to end at 7 a.m. Around 6 a.m., my two new friends and I were walking down a dirt road that wound through the woods. Feeling perfectly safe, we began to sing "We Shall Overcome." Suddenly, an army truck roared up from behind. "Stop!" we heard someone shout. "Stop! Stop! It's OK. The game is over."

We didn't believe them for a second. Instead, we ran like hell into the woods. It soon became apparent that the truck was loaded with "enemy" Rangers. Over my shoulder, I saw them leap out of the vehicle and dash into the woods. It was now a foot race through the puckerbrush. The adrenaline pumped through my body so fast I though my heart would explode. There was absolutely no way I was going to let those guys catch me. I didn't want to find out how much pain they could inflict on me over the next hour.

I must have run like a deer because they didn't catch me. They did, however, capture one of my companions. In the woods of Georgia, vines sometimes grow from one bush to another. These "wait-a-minute" vines can trip anyone who doesn't see them. One of the vines caught my friend's ankle and dropped him hard on the ground. Before he could get up, an enemy soldier had a rifle butt inches from his face threatening to smash his teeth in. Apparently, this Ranger thought he had captured me.

I didn't dare show my face until I was sure it was after 7 o'clock—on *everyone's* watch. I came out of the woods just in time for our scheduled debriefing. The game was over and the Rangers couldn't touch me now. They let me know that they thought I was a coward, that I didn't play by the rules, and that they would look for a chance to get even. From then on, I was singled out for more than the usual amount of harassment and push-ups. By then, though, IOBC was almost over and I managed to limp through the remaining days until graduation.

****

The next stop was army intelligence school at Fort Holabird in Maryland. This was more of a "chalk and talk" school, with lectures about intelligence tactics, the evils of socialism, and the domino theory. (You remember the domino theory, don't you? We had to stop the communists in South Vietnam or the next thing we knew they'd be surfing at Waikiki.) In addition, we also learned such useful skills as how to stab ourselves with a pencil-sized needle in case we became the victim of a gas attack. Personally, this exercise seemed pointless to me. If I was under a real nerve gas attack, I'd be happy to ram a dozen needles into me. But to stab myself just to see how brave I was? No thanks. Not then, not now.

Luckily, the needle-stabbing drill was conducted in a large lecture hall so I was able to fake it. I pinched up a piece of my pants and ran the needle through the cloth. Then I pushed down on the vial and released the liquid all over my leg and pants. When the instructors checked my aisle, they saw the needle sticking up out of my pants and assumed I had done my duty. They never noticed the wet spot on my leg.

Henry Billings

Our education at Fort Holabird had a specific goal. Socialism was bad, not just for us but for everyone else in the world. The notion that this premise might be debatable never occurred to our instructors. Their job was to indoctrinate, not to discuss. I had always thought of socialism as an economic system. It didn't bother me if the Vietnamese, halfway around the world, wanted to practice some sort of collective agriculture. Wasn't that more in line with their ancient traditions, anyway? Didn't the Vietnamese look more to Confucius than to Adam Smith for guidance? Wasn't their group ethic more powerful than any urge to promote the rights of the individual? Wasn't the simple life more valued than a flashy display of wealth? At Holabird, of course, such questions were never entertained. Instead, we got lectures on some of the obvious flaws in *The Communist Manifesto.*

One class featured a captain I'll call "Major Tuck." He had recently returned from a tour in Vietnam as an advisor to the South Vietnamese. He had come back to tell us stories and to convince us just how vital it was to defeat the Vietnamese communists. He spent a lot of time talking about rice. Major Tuck declared that if the communists won the "rice bowl" of Asia, then the communists in China could get enough food to feed all their people. According to Tuck, these well-fed Chinese Reds could then spend all their time developing nuclear weapons and planning how to blow up the United States. It was our job, Tuck told us, to stop them. There was no telling how vile the Chinese would be if their stomachs were full. At one point, I raised my hand and asked a question. "If the Chinese Communists are the real threat, why aren't we fighting them instead of the Vietnamese?"

I don't remember Tuck's exact answer. But I do remember everyone looking at me as if I was some sort of certifiable idiot. Everyone knew that communism was a monolithic threat. If you beat them in one place, you wounded the entire beast. In 1962, General Lyman Lemnitser, who was at the time the Chairman of the Joint Chiefs of Staff, said that Vietnam's fall was a "planned phase in the Communist timetable for world domination." This view was shared by other top military and administration policymakers for years to come.

I had serious doubts about that. I didn't know it at the time, but others shared my skepticism. Many CIA agents, for example, felt that communism wasn't a monolithic bloc. They held that the war in Vietnam was strictly Hanoi's show. It wasn't directed from Moscow or Peking. These CIA agents also felt that the Sino-Soviet split was for real and not, as some top policymakers makers maintained, a plot to deceive the West. Some agents even had doubts about the domino theory. In 1964, the White House asked the CIA to comment on the domino theory. The CIA's Office of National Estimates replied, "We do not believe that the loss of South Vietnam and Laos would be followed by the rapid, successive communization of the other states in the Far East." These voices, however, never had any real impact in the overall direction of American policy.

Another flaw with the "monolithic beast" theory was the intense hatred that most Vietnamese felt toward the Chinese. I didn't learn about this from Major Tuck or anyone else at Fort Holabird. No one there brought up Vietnam's thousand-year struggle against Chinese domination. No one mentioned General Tran Hung Dao, one of the great heroes in Vietnamese history. In 1282, the Chinese had sent a murderous army of 500,000 men into Vietnam. The Vietnamese king considered surrendering to save his people from total destruction. General Tran Hung Dao flatly rejected the idea. He told the king, "If you wish to surrender, order my head to be severed first." The general's courage inspired the king to order an all-out defense of his realm. Although vastly outnumbered, Tran Hung Dao drove the invaders out using hit-and-run guerrilla tactics. He was just one of countless Vietnamese heroes who fought against the Chinese. But to hear Tuck tell it, you would have thought the Vietnamese were dancing with anticipation at the thought of sending surplus

Henry Billings

rice to their buddies north of the border. A little more history and a little less propaganda would have helped everyone at Holabird.

Truth be told, talk of the dangers caused by a Vietnam-China rice flow was the sunny side of the major's lecture. He went on to relate some of his personal experiences in Vietnam. Tuck bragged about questioning a suspected Viet Cong agent in a village square. He told how all the villagers had gathered around him. The VC prisoner was on his knees in front of Tuck. The major grabbed the man's hair and began to interrogate him. At some point, the man spit on Tuck. After wiping the spit off, the major placed the muzzle of his pistol against the man's temple and pulled the trigger. "If I didn't kill him," Major Tuck told his stunned class, "I would have lost face in front of all the villagers." I shuddered to think that this guy was on *our* side. What I didn't know at the time was that this form of summary execution was common on both sides in the Vietnam War.

It was at Fort Holabird in the summer of 1965 that most of us got the news that we would be shipping out to Vietnam. (On July 28, President Lyndon Johnson announced that American troop strength in Vietnam would be increased from 75,000 to 125,000. Even more would go if it was necessary, he declared. Johnson also reported that the monthly draft call would jump from 17,000 to 35,000—the highest since the Korean War. As a nation, we were about to jump into this quagmire with both feet.) For me, it was time to put up or shut up.

Well, that's not exactly true. I was never really going to shut up—my mouth in those days was on automatic pilot. Still, I had to decide whether I would go or find a way out fast. I decided to go. If I had been in the same predicament in 1967 or 1968, I can't say for sure what I would have done. I'd like to think I would have either gone to jail or learned to speak Swedish or sung *O Canada* at all future sporting events.

As things turned out, I probably made the right decision in terms of my own life. I don't think I could ever have made peace with myself if I had run away. In addition, I would have felt I had forfeited the right to comment on the war. Pat Conway, author of *The Great Santini* and *The Lords of Discipline* was in the same fix a few years later. He decided to protest the war and later regretted the decision. He said, "I should have gone and done my duty for my country, then come back and run my mouth. I think that would have been fair. Then my country could have looked at that and said, "OK. He was over there. He did that. He knows what he's talking about and he has the right to talk'."

That was pretty much how I felt at the time. Up to this point in my life, all I had was a bit of book knowledge. Despite the trip to Europe, I hadn't really done much of anything in the real world. This was my chance to see the war up close and personal. So, once again, I was of two minds. On the one hand, I thought that the war was wrong on all levels. But, on the other hand, I wanted to learn from direct experience what I was talking about.

*****

As we prepared to ship off for Vietnam, most of us were pretty clueless. Exactly what we were supposed to do once we got there was a bit of a mystery. No one told us anything. We did, however, hear rumors that we would be assigned as sector intelligence advisors to ARVN (South Vietnamese army) units. 'Oh,' I remember thinking, 'that's just dandy.' I didn't know the first thing about Vietnam and yet I was going to be advising people who have lived there all their lives. Surely that was a joke.

We didn't leave for Vietnam right away. First, we went to Fort Bragg in North Carolina. There I, along with my friends from Holabird, were assigned to the 519th Military Intelligence Battalion. We stayed at Bragg all through the early fall, mostly just waiting and playing golf. At night I often drove with some buddies to the coffeehouses in Fayetteville. Even in the shadows of one of America's biggest army bases, protest songs could already be heard. But they were mild and no one as yet had taken to the streets *en masse* to demonstrate against the war.

The strongest act—at least symbolically—anyone took at this stage was the burning of draft cards. On August 31, President Johnson made that illegal. Under the new law, anyone who burned his draft card could be sent to prison for up to five years. (David Miller, a Catholic pacifist, became famous in the anti-war movement after he publicly burned his draft card and was later sentenced to 30 months in prison.)

At last, in early November, I got my orders. Most of my friends got theirs, too. The 519th MI battalion would be sent as a unit. That meant that we had to go by ship, since we would be bringing all our equipment with us. (Later, our replacements would fly straight to Vietnam.)

We set sail from Charleston, South Carolina in early November. The clock for our one-year tour began to tick as soon as we weighed anchor. That was fine with me. I was in no hurry. 'Hey, captain,' I thought, 'Take your time. Make it a slow boat to Indochina.' In fact, it was slow. Slow and, at least at first, pleasant. There was lots of room to move around and the food was good. We sailed south past communist Cuba, through the Panama Canal and up to Long Beach, California. There we changed to a smaller ship. Several hundred more soldiers from different units were put on with us. We were packed so tight I felt like an immigrant in steerage headed for Ellis Island in 1900. After a few days in port, we headed west across the vast Pacific. To pass our days at sea we played cards, read books, and watched Beach Blanket Bingo movies under the stars at night. The message was clear. Our job was to crush the commies so Annette and Frankie could wiggle their butts safely on beaches in Southern California.

As the days passed, however, I grew bored. I didn't want to sail to Vietnam without stirring up at least a little excitement. So I conducted a Gallup Poll among the junior officers in the 519th. This sounded innocuous enough. But I asked all the hot-button questions. I asked the men their opinions on topics ranging from capital punishment to gun control to mining Haiphong Harbor. This boat-rocking stunt angered the officer who evaluated my on-ship performance. I had done all the petty little duties assigned me during the voyage. But he felt that with my poll, I had damaged morale and questioned authority. He gave me a poor report that went into my personal file. I had flunked the cruise.

On December 23, 1965, the coast of Vietnam appeared on the horizon.

Henry Billings

Chapter 3 ~~ Welcome to Saigon

"When you open the door to the breeze, the dirt comes in too."
—old Vietnamese proverb

On December 20th, the Viet Cong (VC) marked the 5th anniversary of the NLF (National Liberation Front). The NLF was created by the North Vietnamese to wage war in South Vietnam. What better way to celebrate the occasion than to blow up a few Americans? We got wind of a rumor that our ship was a target. That news added a little spice to our sail up the Saigon River. Suddenly we felt like floating ducks. Welcome to Saigon.

From the VC's point of view, sinking our ship would have been a great gift to Uncle Ho. Imagine blowing up a shipload of American spies before they even set foot on Vietnamese soil! I'm happy to report, however, that it didn't happen. The military sent experts out to our ship as we approached the port. These guys dropped percussion grenades into the river, sending water spouts high into the air. Many of us leaned over the railing expecting to see a dead body or two bob to the surface. None did.

Still, VC terrorism wasn't an empty threat. The VC had already compiled an impressive track record. If we had any lingering doubts, all we had to do was hear the story of the My Canh floating restaurant which we sailed past on the Saigon River. The My Canh, known for its terrific food and fine views across the river, was a favorite American watering hole. Shortly before we arrived, the VC bombed the restaurant, killing nine Americans and more than 20 Vietnamese. (I quickly made a mental note to myself: Don't eat there, no matter how good the food is said to be. Later, however, I changed my mind. The My

VIETNAM FOLLIES
A Memoir of an Intelligence Officer

Canh, it turned out, was only marginally more dangerous than other places in Saigon and the food really was pretty terrific.)

Killing their own people had never posed a moral dilemma for the Viet Cong. If they wanted to make a political point, they didn't hesitate to slit a countryman's throat. Murdering Saigon-appointed rural leaders was a VC specialty. But in the case of the My Canh restaurant, they had killed many totally innocent people. The VC later issued a weak apology. Even then they couldn't resist tacking on a sober warning: "So sorry, it was a mistake. But you must stay away from the Americans. We want to kill more of them. If you are with them, we'll kill you, too."

The Viet Cong mostly targeted American installations in Saigon. From December 1964 to December 1965, they struck whenever and wherever they pleased. For example, they bombed the Brink Hotel, where U.S. officers lived. They also attacked the American embassy and the Kinh Do cinema, which was patronized mostly by Americans. During my first week in Vietnam, the VC lobbed grenades into three open trucks carrying Americans, wounding 18. They also planted bombs in the Rainbow Bar and the Playboy Club.

Americans and Saigonese took countermeasures to lower the risk of terrorism. To prevent the Viet Cong from chucking grenades into restaurants and bars, owners installed screen barriers. (I quickly learned to pick restaurant seats that let me keep my back to the wall and my eye on the door.) All buses screened in their windows, too. American-occupied establishments, such as the Rex Hotel, had sandbag barriers topped by barbed wire and patrolled by well-armed guards in flak jackets. Guards searched Vietnamese visitors before they could enter these places. The Vietnamese also had to leave their ID cards at the desk with security guards. General William Westmoreland took VC threats seriously. During my first week "in country", he ordered a strict dawn-to-dusk curfew for all Americans. Such curfews would become a regular feature for

Americans stationed in Saigon. Westmoreland imposed them whenever the threat of VC violence seemed particularly high.

Still, if the Viet Cong wanted to kill a few Americans, they could always find a way to do it. Some of them were quite creative. Although we never crossed paths, the legendary Saigon Sally was on everyone's mind. Rumors told of her riding on the back on a Honda motor scooter and taking pot shots at passing Americans. I never put ice in my drinks at a Vietnamese restaurant because—so the story went—the VC controlled the icehouses and sometimes put small bits of broken glass into the ice. On one occasion a street vendor asked a passing GI to hold a bunch of balloons for a second. The neighborly American obliged. The vendor quickly walked away and the balloons exploded. The Viet Cong rigged black-market cigarette lighters to explode when lighted. They even carried poisonous hypodermic needles that they could jab into an American leg on a crowded street.

But, for me, the most feared terrorist device was the claymore mine. Right after I arrived in Vietnam, the Viet Cong used a claymore mine to kill several Americans who were waiting at a bus stop. Someone put a claymore mine on the back of a nearby bicycle. Then he or she walked a safe distance away and detonated the mine. The VC didn't make their own claymore mines. They stole them from us. Obviously, I had no interest in dying. But I had less than no interest in having my flesh ripped apart by a weapon I helped to pay for.

Life or death: it was mostly a matter of chance. Saigon was crawling with VC agents—as the Tet Offensive would later prove. You couldn't walk any street in Saigon without passing at least a half dozen VC agents or sympathizers. After the war, the truth came out. All sorts of well-known and trusted Vietnamese confessed, "Oh, by the way, I was an NLF operative all the time." Some ran big businesses; some served in the South Vietnamese army; some even worked as journalists for western media.

VIETNAM FOLLIES
A Memoir of an Intelligence Officer

One famous example was Colonel Pham Xuan An. This NLF undercover agent fooled everyone. An was so trusted and respected that he rose to become a full-fledged correspondent for *Time* magazine. Here was a witty and talented man who genuinely loved Americans. He came to the United States under the auspices of the army and the recommendation of counterinsurgency icon Edward G. Lansdale. He fell in love with the United States and its people. He would later say that Americans had done much good in South Vietnam. He saw us as mostly kind and honest in our dealings with Vietnamese. He recognized that we brought with us a sense of justice, fair play, and respect for the worth of the individual. (Starting in September 1967, the Army ordered every soldier to carry a pocket card called Nine Rules. Some examples which might have impressed An: Rule #1: Remember we are guests here: We make no demands and seek no special treatment. Rule # 2: Join with the people! Understand their life, use phrases from their language and honor their customs and laws. Rule # 3: Treat women with politeness and respect. Rule # 9: Above all else you are members of the U.S. Military Forces on a difficult mission, responsible for all your official and personal actions. Reflect honor upon yourself and the United States of America.) According to his friend *New York Times* reporter Henry Kamm, An gets almost misty-eyed when talking about American virtues. And yet he was working for the other side all along. Later, after the war, the communists even promoted him to the rank of general. If we couldn't get a guy like Pham Xuan An to fight on our side, well, then maybe there was something was wrong with our policy.

There were also plenty of low-level sympathizers. At first, I thought the vast majority of Saigonese as well as Vietnamese were on our side or, at worst, neutral. At Fort Holabird, the so-called intelligence experts told us that there were about 10,000 hard-core Viet Cong and about 50,000 part-time guerrillas. Those figures were woefully out of date even in the summer of

Henry Billings

1965. Maybe, just maybe, they were close to the strength numbers in 1960 when the National Liberation Front was founded.

By 1965, the actual number of Viet Cong was much, much higher. In hindsight, this was typical of our intelligence in Vietnam. We constantly underestimated the true manpower of our adversary. Such mistakes would cost thousands of American lives in the years ahead. It's one thing to fight an enemy force of, say, 5,000 troops. It is quite another to head into battle expecting an enemy force of 5,000 only to discover that there are actually 10,000 troops arrayed against you.

Some people joked that "military intelligence" was an oxymoron. I laughed, too. But I didn't really believe it. In retrospect, I can't believe how naïve I was. If I had given it more thought, I might have remembered all the major intelligence blunders from Pearl Harbor to the North Korean invasion of South Korea to the Bay of Pigs. Intelligence experts missed them all. In Vietnam, we would add to that miserable record by playing a game of self-deception. Basically, we cooked the books on everything from enemy troop strength to the effectiveness of our bombing programs to an assessment of enemy morale. It was all done to maintain the illusion of success. We were our own worst enemy.

*****

The Viet Cong could have killed me any time someone thought it was a good idea. It was that simple. My local barber, for example, could have done it. As a soldier, I was supposed to get my hair cut once a week. Once every two weeks sounded better to me. Even so, that made close to 25 trips to the barber's chair. Since I was always trying out a different shop, the odds are slim that I was always in friendly hands. At some point, a VC barber must have held a razor to my throat, dreaming of Sweeney Todd. Of course, slitting my throat would have been a

VIETNAM FOLLIES
A Memoir of an Intelligence Officer

bit messy. But any barber could have easily and neatly broken my neck. All Vietnamese barbers had this little thing they did after cutting someone's hair. First, they cracked all their client's fingers. Then, taking the person's head firmly in both hands, they snapped it quickly, cracking, but not breaking, the neck. I wasn't expecting it the first time and—I'm not ashamed to admit—it scared the hell out of me. Now suppose the barber – no longer interested in getting a tip—changed the pressure points just a bit. It would have been a nice clean way to either paralyze or kill a man.

If you believed the legend, there was a Viet Cong woman who disguised herself as a prostitute. Now I have no doubt that at least some of the city's hookers were VC, but this one was something special. Her dedication to her cause went far beyond the call of duty since, as the rumor had it, she lined her vagina with sharp objects, usually said to be razor blades.

Still, on balance, I think the Viet Cong were second-rate terrorists. If they wanted to really demoralize the United States early in the war, they could have done it. One day in 1966, the VC launched a mortar attack on Tan Son Nhut Airport. They destroyed a number of warplanes on the ground with precision fire. The shells blew the cockpits clean off the bodies, making the planes look like dead fish with their heads removed. One of the shells hit a barrack, killing an American while he slept in his bunk. He was just one wake-up call from getting out alive. The next morning he would have caught a 707 for home. His death shocked many of us. Somehow it didn't seem fair that a guy could make it 364 days and then get killed. Dying was bad enough. But to be so close to going home was really tough.

And then it occurred to me. Why didn't the VC shoot down some of these 707s? As the mortar strike clearly showed, they had the ability to penetrate the airport. So it would have been child's play to knock out an airliner as it rambled down the runway. One rocket would have destroyed the plane and all the people on board. Imagine killing a hundred or so soldiers on the

Henry Billings

way home. Now that would have been demoralizing! I have no idea why the VC never blew a commercial jet out of the sky. (They may have tried once and failed. In 1964, a .30-caliber bullet ripped through an oil pipeline in an engine of the Pan American World Airways Boeing 707 but the pilot managed to land the safely. The speculation at the time was that the VC wanted to kill Secretary of Defense Robert S. McNamara who was to arrive the same day on a 707. The VC hired the wrong travel agent. McNamara was on a different plane.) Wouldn't such a large-scale act of terrorism have sickened Americans? How would we have handled it? Would we have launched a massive bombing of North Vietnam population centers like the bombing raids in 1972? Or would the anti-war movement have moved off campus much earlier?

****

The threat of terrorism was but one of the many faces of Saigon. Being in Asia was a new experience for me. I knew I would see and smell things that I had never seen or smelled in the United States. A choking blanket of exhaust fumes from motorcycles and buses and jeeps was something I expected. I knew, too, that Saigon would be overcrowded—perhaps the most densely packed city in the world, despite most of the houses being only one or two stories high. And I knew there would be slums.

But other things really shook me. I had never seen a woman going to the bathroom on the street. That happened all the time in Saigon. Women would just squat down on a curb and do their business. No furtive glances. It was considered natural. In my opinion, that was over the top. To me, a little night soil might have been OK in the rice paddies, but it had limited value on the streets where people walked. I never saw a man take a dump in the streets but men would urinate freely in public. This one-two punch gave many city streets the smell of a toilet. Most of these open-air defecators, I suspect, were rural refugees who were swelling the population of "The Pearl of the Orient." (In 1966, maybe as many as one million peasants fled to Saigon and other towns and cities—the real "strategic hamlets" of this war.)

Garbage overwhelmed the city. People who might remember the New York City garbage workers' strike should have been in Saigon to really understand how bad it could get. At the end of the street where I lived, there was a permanent mountain of rotting garbage. You could walk by it after dark, throw a rock or stick into the pile, and watch rats the size of small dogs dart from one side of the pile to the other. As the months passed, the pile seemed to get higher and the rats bolder. Apparently, no one took responsibility to clean the filth from streets. Saigon is laced with rivers and canals. People threw or dumped everything in them. Then they built thatched huts on stilts out over the brackish filth.

Although we had been warned not to go near the any of the slums, I wanted to see what they were like anyway. So one night I strolled with a friend to explore one slum no more than 200 yards from my house. A couple of waterlogged boards served as the walkway between two stilt houses. We could feel the thin wood sagging under our weight. Water seeped out of the wood around our shoes. Our greatest fear was that we might slip and tumble into the cesspool of a river. In my mind it would have been like falling into a chemical vat. I was sure my skin would liquify like the monster at the end of some "B" horror movie.

The older residents stared at us, wondering what we wanted. But they remained silent. Girls over the age of 12 looked at us nervously as if we had come for them. I could only take an hour or two of this. It seemed that we—the United States—should do something to help these people. But what? It was estimated that the aid money we sent to Vietnam, after it filtered through all the cronies and the bureaucracy, was less than $1 per person per year.

Henry Billings

*****

Before we left the States, army doctors had loaded us with of vaccines against tropical diseases. After we arrived in Vietnam, we got another round. No one complained. We wanted as much protection as western medicine could provide.

The poor Vietnamese were, if you'll excuse the expression, dropping like flies. In the best of times, Saigon wasn't the healthiest location in the world. This torrid city was built on a low mud bank. Its streets turn into rivers during the rainy season. During the war, other problems plagued it as well. Overcrowding, poor drainage, piled-up garbage, plus the intense heat and the mosquitoes led to very high rates of malaria, dysentery, cholera, leprosy, typhoid, and other assorted diseases such as smallpox and bubonic plague which I thought had been wiped out. It was estimated that at least 10% of the population over the age of ten had a form of tuberculosis. The South Vietnamese government did next to nothing to help the sick.

We were not supposed to drink the water. No one had to tell us that. But they did tell us that we shouldn't even brush our teeth with tap water. (I looked for maggots flowing out of the tap but didn't see any.) Every few days I filled my canteen with clean water from the army supply at Tan Son Nhut and used that to brush my teeth. Going to the bathroom in Vietnam was a new experience for me. I was OK so long as I didn't lose my balance squatting over the hole in the floor. It was always safe to eat and drink at army facilities. But on the streets and in the local restaurants, it was a different story. We all assumed we would "get the runs." I was so uptight I didn't have a bowel movement for nearly a week. I guess I was afraid that once I started, I'd never be able to stop. There would be plenty of times in the coming months when a toilet, any toilet at all, was the most comforting place to be.

The guys in the field, the ones doing the real fighting, called us "Saigon warriors." Most of us didn't even carry guns. Our war was an antiseptic one. We never really got our hands dirty. To us, the war was like a TV drama. We could see it any time we wanted. But instead of flicking the dial, we took the elevator to the top of the Caravelle Hotel for dinner. Its rooftop terrace was a popular hangout for journalists and us "Saigon warriors." The real war was right there across the Saigon River in living color. You could be working on your fifth bottle of beer while watching the tracer bullets streaking red through the damp night air a mile or so away. Soldiers on both sides were dying in the dark while I was being asked what I'd like to have for dessert.

Another face of Saigon, when there was no curfew, was the nightlife. Saigon in the early 60's was a weird mix of Puritanism and debauchery. Madame Ngo Dinh Nhu, President Diem's sister-in-law, passed all sorts of laws outlawing fun. Before the 1963 coup, which ended in the deaths of her husband and brother-in-law, this devout Roman Catholic had banned abortions, outlawed all forms of contraceptives, and made divorce a crime. Saigon's "first lady" had also banned beauty contests, boxing, and dancing. Women were not allowed to wear padded bras. (The local police, dubbed White Mice because of their white uniforms, had the duty of enforcing the edict.) Madame Nhu fled Vietnam after the coup. To most Vietnamese, it was good riddance. But a handful of Vietnamese who shared some of her sentiments remained in segments of the Saigon population.

By 1965, Saigon was an open city. Like Havana before Castro, anything and everything was for sale. The black market flourished. Every week huge cargo ships from the United States brought supplies for the GIs. We may have been at war, but that was no reason not to have all the comforts of home. So the Post Exchange was filled with TVs, Japanese radios, Corn Flakes, wine, beer, and magazines, including the latest issue of *Playboy*. But much of this stuff never made it to the PX. It was stolen right off the dock or later from a storage building. So if you wanted, say, an Swiss army knife or a Nikon camera at a real bargain price, you could buy it on the street from a Vietnamese vendor. Even the garbage trucks sent to help pick up the city's trash never made it past the docks. They were stripped clean of all useful parts by local thugs before the people in charge of garbage removal could drive them away.

If I bought anything on the local market, I was supposed to pay in piasters, the local Vietnamese currency. The piaster, however, was highly inflationary. So sometimes the vendors wanted MPCs (Military Payment Certificates). MPCs held their value better, at least on a day-to-day basis. Every six months or so, though, the U.S. military would change the MPCs. It was a bit like changing the play money in *Monopoly* for the play money in *Life*. Every American had to turn in all old MCPs for the new script. It all had to be done quickly—in just a few days. Thus, by simple decree, the old MPCs were rendered worthless. The United States did this to punish black marketeers. Any Vietnamese stuck with soon-to-be-worthless MPCs under a straw mattress had to find a GI to sell them to fast—at a very sharp discount.

The Vietnamese vendors couldn't ask for dollars. No American was supposed to have any greenbacks on him. When we arrived in country, we had to turn in all our dollars in exchange for MPCs of equal face value. The MPCs functioned just like dollars on base or at the PX. So for everyday living we didn't need dollars.

Both Americans and Vietnamese played money games. I got a first-hand taste of money laundering a few days after my arrival. My mother sent me a Christmas card with $20 inside. I had already turned in my greenbacks, so I stuffed the bill deep in my wallet. The next day I was riding the elevator of the Majestic Hotel. Suddenly, the operator stopped the car between floors. "Do you have any dollars?" he asked.

Not knowing how to respond, I hesitated at first. But I saw this as a chance to get rid of the bill. "I have a twenty," I said. The man reached into his pocket and took out twice the amount

VIETNAM FOLLIES
A Memoir of an Intelligence Officer

of the official exchange rate. In short, I got $40 worth of piasters for my $20.

Ma Billings didn't raise a fool. I saw instantly the potential for riches. I could easily have made a lot of money. All I had to do was take the $40 which the operator had given me to an army bank and exchange it for $40 in MPCs. Next I'd buy a $40 postal money order made out to my mother in the United States. She then would cash it for $40 and the money back to me in dollar bills. There were lots of people like my friend in the elevator who desperately wanted hard currency and would give me two or three times the face value back in piasters. Also, the U.S. army had several places in Saigon where I could exchange money and buy postal money orders. So I could have kept doubling or tripling my money indefinitely. In the early days, the risk was small if you limited your activity to about, say, $500 dollars a day.

Still, the Boy Scout in me warned against it. Laundering money was, of course, illegal and there was the chance that I'd get caught. (In 1966, Navy Captain Archie Kuntze, a highly-decorated World War II and Korean War veteran and the unofficial "American mayor of Saigon", was brought before a court-martial for illegally converting Vietnamese currency into dollars.) Also, if I didn't watch out, I could get ripped off. More than one GI got nothing more than a neatly-wrapped package of cut-up newspaper in exchange for his American cash.) But the trump card in my mind was the question of what my dollars would ultimately be used to buy. In most cases, American cash represented an exit strategy for middle-class Vietnamese. If South Vietnam went to hell in a handbasket, at least these people could flee the country with real money. But I believed that some of the money might be used to buy guns for the VC. I didn't want the blood of an American soldier on my hands even though I would never know about it. For me, that was enough of a reason to write my mother and tell her not to send me any more cash.

Henry Billings

****

Saigon back then was like Bangkok today. It had the smell of sex about it. Every day, it seemed, a new bar was opening up around Tu Do Street (Freedom Street) with a revealing name such as Golden Cock, the Flame, or the Butterfly Bar. These bars were ably patrolled by about 8,000 bar girls. Some wore Western-style miniskirts. The more provocative ones wore *ao dais*, the traditional Vietnamese silk pant suit. An *ao dai* covers everything and hides nothing. That dress may have been the single most important reason why some guys actually volunteered for a second or third tour of duty in Vietnam. One pilot said with a grin, "Listen, we gotta save these girls from Communism."

Someone said that 95% of the girls were prostitutes. Whoever dreamt up that number was just being kind. The reality was that any virgin who found employment in these bars didn't remain chaste for long. Virginity simply wasn't operationally viable.

Whenever you walked into one of these bars, the girls would rush to greet you. "Where you from? "What your name?" "You like me?" "How long you been in Saigon?" It was in its own way an amusing ritual. If you wanted the companionship of one girl, you would buy her a glass of "Saigon Tea." It was just colored water or iced tea but it was priced like a shot of whiskey. A few soldiers once protested the high price by organizing the STIF (Saigon Tea is Fini) committee. The movement was doomed from the start. After all, Saigon Tea was just a means to an end and the end had a relatively inflexible demand curve.

In theory, we were in Vietnam to win the *hearts and minds* of the people. In practice, we stole their women. Vietnamese males were, understandably, angry when their girlfriends brushed them aside for Americans. As foreigners we no doubt had a certain exotic appeal to the women. (The reverse was certainly true.) They may have laughed at our big noses and pale skin, but still I always felt as though they really liked us. No one could ever be absolutely sure since we also had much more money than the local competition. The poor Vietnamese males didn't stand a chance. For that matter, they didn't have much of a chance trying to get a taxi if a nearby American was also looking. Many Vietnamese must have felt a bit like the British felt during World War II after the American arrived. The Brits were fond of say, "The trouble with the Americans is they're overpaid, oversexed and—over here!"

The GI-meets-Vietnamese-girl scenario undermined the Vietnamese family, as well. What father could demand filial piety from a daughter who earned 10 times as much as he did? He, too, might work for the Americans on a construction project or as a domestic servant. But his pay paled in comparison to what any bar girl could earn in Saigon. So there were plenty of reasons for the Vietnamese to hate us Americans. Some of us, of course, fooled ourselves into thinking that we were liberating the Vietnamese from communism. But in everyday life, most Vietnamese saw us as just another foreign invader—one who controlled the government, ran the war, and destroyed Vietnamese values. Overall, our behavior was not the best way to win the hearts and minds of the people.

Still, in a perverse way some Vietnamese profited from our presence. By taking over the war, we freed some young Vietnamese men from the obligation of fighting for their own country. And we were doing exactly what we shouldn't have been doing. We were fighting in their place. Robert McNamara in his mea culpa memoir *In Retrospect: The Tragedy and Lessons of Vietnam* wrote, "If the South Vietnamese were to be saved, they had to win the war themselves." What a laugh. Why should they fight when we were more than willing to do it for them?

I remember being sickened by a conversation I had with one Vietnamese bar owner. He was about 20 years old and looked physically fit. "Do you want Ho Chi Minh to take over South Vietnam?" I asked him one night.

"Oh, no," he answered. "Ho Chi Minh bad—he number 10. (In Vietnamese, Number 1 was very good – the best, while "Number 10" was very bad—the worst. In extreme cases of unpopularity, someone might be called "Number 10 thousand," or in Vietnamese shorthand, "Number 10 Thou." That was more like a curse.)

"Then why don't you join the army and fight him?"

"No," he snapped. "You fight war. I run bar."

If I had any second thoughts about the mistake the U. S. was making in South Vietnam, that young man cured me. In all likelihood, he was a draft dodger. Even before the United States had a big problem with men dodging the draft, it was a common practice in South Vietnam. By the end of 1965, for example, it was estimated that over 230,000 Vietnamese youths had evaded the draft. In their defense, these young men had no compelling reason to demonstrate loyalty to their government. South Vietnam as a nation was a fiction. It was a hodgepodge of different religions, races, languages, and cultures. There was no "common good" and every one of these young men knew it. They had no sense of patriotism or sacrifice for the entity of South Vietnam. The only real loyalty most of them had was to their families.

****

Our leaders told us that we were in Vietnam to defend freedom and democracy. That notion didn't work even as a joke. Since the creation of South Vietnam after the Geneva Accords in 1954, the United States government bent over backwards to deceive itself. During a 1961 tour to South Vietnam, Vice President Lyndon B. Johnson compared Ngo Dinh Diem to Winston Churchill. I guess he meant they were both short and fat. When journalist Stanley Karnow asked Johnson to defend his characterization, the Vice President said, "Shit, Diem's the only boy we got out there."

Americans begged Diem to hold elections even though we knew they would be rigged. We wanted him to look democratic. Appearances counted. But, so too, did a little subtlety. "You don't need 99% of the vote," we told him. "What you want is about 80%." It wouldn't play well in the United States to showcase the spectacle of an unopposed victory.

Diem, the autocrat, would have nothing to do with this charade. He wanted no opposition. None at all. It didn't matter how small or how loyal or how anti-communist the opposition might be; it had to be weeded out. Some democracy. In the end, when Diem refused to play ball, we turned a blind eye to his assassination. We should have learned an easy lesson. You can't give away democracy. You can't go up to foreigners and say, "Hey, here's some democracy. Go home and practice free elections." People have to develop democratic institutions on their own. And it doesn't happen overnight. After all, it took the western world more than two thousand years to develop its own democratic institutions. It should have come as no surprise that with no democratic traditions, Vietnam—North and South—remained authoritarian.

The generals who followed Diem in South Vietnam did nothing to hide the fact that they couldn't care less what the average Vietnamese thought. The fix was in on all elections. The army guarded the polling booths to insure that 150% of the people voted the right way. The press was censored. Every day you could pick up the paper and see big blank spaces where the censors had cut articles they didn't like. Any South Vietnamese citizen with the courage to speak out against the regime of the moment was tossed in jail and forgotten. Between Diem's fall in November 1963 and my arrival in December 1965, South Vietnam had nine different governments. One general's tanks rolled through Saigon to overthrow another general. Dean Rusk, Secretary of State under Kennedy and Johnson said, "The United

States has not provided massive assistance to South Vietnam, in military equipment, economic resources, and personnel in order to subsidize continuing quarrels among South Vietnam's leaders." That, of course, is exactly what we did.

****

Back in America, the debate over the Vietnam War focused on one central question: was it a civil war or was it an invasion of one sovereign nation by another sovereign nation? Those who opposed the war, like me, said it was a civil war and therefore none of our business. On the other hand, those who favored U. S. intervention argued that North Vietnam had crossed an international border to attack a neighbor, not unlike Germany attacking Poland in 1939.

Who was right? And could they prove their case? Most Americans wanted to do the right thing. Minding our own business was the right thing to do. But so, too, was resisting aggression. Public support for the war turned on this question.

On February 27, 1965, the State Department issued a White Paper on Vietnam entitled "Aggression from the North." Objectivity wasn't the goal, so it didn't pull any rhetorical punches The opening line went for the kill. "South Vietnam is fighting for its life against a brutal campaign of terror and armed attack inspired, directed, supplied, and controlled by the Communist regime in Hanoi." Clearly, this was no civil war. The White Paper continued: "Above all, the war in Vietnam is not a spontaneous and local rebellion against the established government… In Vietnam a Communist government has set out deliberately to conquer a sovereign people in a neighboring state…their aggression is as real as that of an invading army."

The White Paper went on to detail "massive evidence" to prove its case. Its main points were that the vast majority of communist soldiers came from North Vietnam and that they were armed by their communist brothers in China and the Soviet

VIETNAM FOLLIES
A Memoir of an Intelligence Officer

Union. According to the White Paper, "The United States has responded to the appeals of the Government of the Republic of Vietnam for help in this defense of the freedom and independence of its land and its people."

The independent journalist and publisher I. F. Stone responded in his March 8th issue of *I. F. Stone's Weekly.* To him, it *was* a civil war. Stone ridiculed the White Paper for its many misleading statements and glaring omissions. For example, of the 15,100 weapons captured from the Viet Cong, only 179 turned out to be communist-made. All the others were either captured from us or purchased through some third party. Also, by checking their home provinces, Stone discovered that only 6 of the 7,000 or so Viet Cong who infiltrated into the south during 1964 were ethnic North Vietnamese. The others did infiltrate. But they were South Vietnamese who had gone north after the Geneva Accords of 1954.

The White Paper concluded by saying that Hanoi's aggression was "directly contrary to the Geneva Accords of 1954." Stone pointed out that it failed to mention the canceled election of 1956, which was supposed to reunite the country under one government. South Vietnam figured it would lose the election, so it refused to participate. That was a violation of the Geneva Accords. The White Paper also failed to acknowledge our own violations. One such violation was entering into a military alliance with South Vietnam. Another was sending more military advisors than allowed under the accords.

So was it a civil war or an invasion? As an academic debate, Stone won by a TKO. But in the real world it didn't really matter. The real issue was that Ho Chi Minh was a communist. In his autobiography he even admitted to sleeping with a copy of *Das Kapital* under his pillow. (Not my choice certainly. *Fanny Hill* maybe.) So American policy treated him like an invader. This was how we justified the war that we wanted. We felt we could beat this bite-size commie and thereby set an example for all the other communists in the Third World.

Henry Billings

Over time, Ho Chi Minh made the State Department's case. In 1964, the overwhelming majority of enemy soldiers were South Vietnamese. By 1969, the majority of enemy soldiers were North Vietnamese. Slowly, the North took over the war effort.

After the war ended, North Vietnamese control over South Vietnam was complete. Hoping to create an egalitarian paradise, Marxist-Leninists from the north quickly turned Vietnam into an economic Bangladesh and a political gulag. It took them many years to realize their tragic mistake. It was only in 1995 that General Vo Nguyen Giap confessed to Stanley Karnow, "Marx was a great analyst, but he never gave us a formula for running a country."

The post-war situation was so bad for many ex-VC that they joined the "boat people," risking their lives in an attempt to flee their homeland. So in the end, if there was a "civil war," it was between the hard-core communists in the North and the soft-core communists of the South.

VIETNAM FOLLIES
A Memoir of an Intelligence Officer

Chapter 4 ~~ Settling In

The Americans thought that the more bombs they dropped, the quicker we would fall to our knees and surrender. But the bombs heightened rather than dampened our spirit.
—Ton That Tung, Ho Chi Minh's personal physician

After disembarking in Saigon, the Army drove us by bus to the outskirts of town, where we spent a week staring at each other in communal tents at Tan Son Nhut Airport and wondering what the Army was going to do with us. With the city under a temporary curfew, we couldn't go much of anywhere other than the latrine and mess tent. Most of us did, however, get to the Bob Hope Christmas Show in another part of Tan Son Nhut on the afternoon of Christmas Eve. There I sat on the ground with some friends, smoking, drinking cold beers, and trying to get used to the idea that I was now at war – well, you know what I mean— half the way around the world. If the rest of my tour was like this, I thought, I might recommend it to others.

Hope brought his usual entourage of blonde Hollywood starlets, a big band, and over-the-hill second bananas. The show mixed musical numbers, some dancing, and a few comedy skits. But the real attraction was Hope's standup routine. He never made fun of individuals. Instead, he joked about Army food, insects, the tropical heat, the anti-war movement. I cringed when Hope suggested one way to beat the Viet Cong was to donate hippie blood to them. But most of the guys lapped it up.

At the time, I didn't like Bob Hope much. He was a war hawk, much too gung-ho for my taste. But, despite our opposing views on the war, I grew to admire him. After all, Hope didn't have to visit the troops. He could have stayed in California

Henry Billings

playing golf in Palm Springs. But he came anyway and always. He did his show during World War II, traveling to the European and Pacific theaters, sometimes doing four or five performances a day while constantly coming up with new material for the locale. He did it during the Korean War, freezing his butt off half the time. Now he was doing it in South Vietnam. And, unlike some celebrities who entertained the troops, he didn't just go to the fortified posts. Hope ventured into harm's way countless times to generate a few laughs for the men far from home.

Christmas Eve was notable for something else. Not only was there a brief 30-hour truce in South Vietnam, but President Johnson called for a halt to Rolling Thunder, the bombing campaign over North Vietnam. Some people thought that this "peace offensive" might actually end the war. Administration officials, including Vice President Hubert Humphrey and Secretary of State Dean Rusk, were running from this country to that country telling friends and foes alike that the United States was willing to talk and that we had no desire for a permanent presence in South Vietnam.

Now that the communists in Hanoi had a taste of American air power, the reasoning went, they would come to their senses and agree to a negotiated settlement. Johnson's "14 points" had such items as a willingness to negotiate without any conditions, a promised regional development program which would include North Vietnam, and the prospect for a united Vietnam "by the free decision of their people." Lyndon Johnson had laid out this plan in a speech he gave at Johns Hopkins University earlier in the year. He, the ultimate wheeler-dealer, figured that if he could just get the Communists to sit down with him, he could simply talk them into ending the war. But the Vietnamese Communists proved to be far less pliable than Senate Republicans.

Still, I briefly allowed myself to think that I might luck out of this war the way my father had lucked out of World War I. My dad reported to Fort Devens for active duty on November 8,

1918. The war ended three days later. He had just enough time to get a haircut and try on his new uniform.

But no such luck for me. Ho Chi Minh refused to budge. He called the American initiative a "trick" and used the bombing lull to send more men and supplies south. The cold shoulder from Hanoi ended what was probably our last best chance for peace before the slaughter began again in earnest and on a massive scale. On January 31, Johnson took his offer off the table and renewed the bombing. No longer dangling his 14 carrots, he began talking about "nailing that coonskin to the wall."

As someone who had no interest in "winning" the war, it was really none of my business. Nevertheless, it seemed to me that we were more interested in "signaling" the enemies than in defeating them. The Johnson administration, which lacked a clearly-defined strategic objective, was obsessed with sending "signals" to North Vietnam and China. If you don't talk, we'll do this or that. We'd bomb and then we'd talk and then we'd bomb some more and then we'd talk some more. I thought that traditional military strategy called for kicking butt first and taking down names and addresses later. You weren't supposed to keep asking "how much is enough?" When you saw the white flag flying over Hanoi, then you'd know for sure that it was enough. But, as I said, this was none of my business.

****

I spent Christmas day like everyone else—opening packages and letters from home. After 40 days at sea without so much as a postcard, the mail had finally caught up with us. My sister Joan had notified the *Boston Herald-American* that I was on my way to Vietnam. The paper sponsored a campaign for school kids to write the men in Vietnam. After my name was printed in the paper, about 100 kids wrote me to say what a wonderful job I was doing defending freedom and, in a few cases, killing the bad guys. I wasn't doing either of these things but it was nice of these kids to support me anyway. I also got hundreds of cookies, candy bars and other goodies from every relative from Massachusetts to Nova Scotia.

Mostly, I gave the sweets to Vietnamese children who appeared out of nowhere every day at the wire fence that surrounded our tents. Long after the war was over, that was the one image I cherished most—an American soldier handing out chewing gum and chocolate bars. It was the image we presented to the world when we and our Allies liberated Western Europe during World War II. We didn't bring fire and blood to the civilians. We didn't rape the women. Instead, we brought smiles and candy. But I was living in the past. South Vietnam wasn't Belgium and Saigon wasn't Paris.

****

For the first week, no one seemed to know what to do with us. (I, for one, thought that if no one wanted us, I would happily go home for reassignment to Germany.) But that was just the way the army worked. Soldiers had an expression for it—hurry up and wait. Someone probably knew what we would be doing. It was just that no one bothered to tell us.

At last we got our orders. The army didn't want me to be a sector intelligence officer after all. My reaction, like Johnny Carson on the *Tonight Show*, was to snap my fingers and mutter "Damn!" while a big grin spread across my face. I was told instead to report to the Research and Analysis Branch of the 519th Military Intelligence Battalion which was stationed just on the other side of Tan Son Nhut airport. Many of my buddies got the same assignment. This tour, I thought, might not be so bad after all.

Our leader, Colonel Gilliland, called us his "intellectual thoroughbreds." Say what? There had to be some mistake. I had been a business management major at a state university. I didn't even graduate cum laude, thanks to my "C" in ROTC after the socialist campaign button fiasco. So how I landed a job among "intellectual thoroughbreds" was a mystery. I guess God does watch over fools and little children. Almost everyone else in my unit, however, lived up to Gilliland's gilt-edged billing. Most of them had gone to an Ivy League school (Harvard, mostly) or had an advanced degree. Two had their law degree and one had his doctorate in political science. To borrow a phrase used elsewhere, we were the "best and the brightest."

Ivy League graduates, of course, would soon become an anomaly in Vietnam. As the anti-war movement heated up, Ivy Leaguers and many others tended to avoid the army altogether. Draft evading became something of a national sport. And, interestingly, it became socially acceptable. There had been no Fort Sumter or Pearl Harbor. No one sank the *Maine*. No one threatened our shores. The Viet Cong were an unseen as well as largely unknown enemy. For the overwhelming majority of Americans, the war had no impact on their lives at all. It was business as usual. There were no gas lines, no ration stamps, no "meatless" days, no savings bond rallies. We were so wealthy as a nation we could afford guns *and* butter. So for many white middle-class young men, everything was fine so long as Uncle Sam didn't crook his finger in their direction.

Thanks to huge loopholes in the draft law, the war would be fought increasingly by blacks, Hispanics, and poor white rural kids. And they were young. The average age of an American in Vietnam was 19. Blacks ended up disproportionately in combat units. Early in the war they made up about 11% of the Vietnam force. But in 1965 and 1966, they suffered well over 20% of the casualties. The situation got so bad that black leaders protested to President Johnson and he ordered black participation in combat units cut back. Hispanics suffered a similar fate but to a lesser degree. Rural states also took a disproportional hit. For example, West Virginia had a death rate of 42 per 100,000 population while New York's death rate was only 22. New Mexico, Wyoming, Oklahoma, and Montana all had death rates over 35. Rhode Island, Delaware, Connecticut, and Massachusetts all had death rates under 24.

In short, the rich and the college-educated found a way out. Some went into the Peace Corps. Some discovered a previously hidden desire to go on to graduate school. Some got married, reminding girls to "Say yes to the guy who says no." (By mid-1966, these so-called "Johnson husbands" had to get their wives pregnant to be certain of avoiding an A-1 draft status.) Others faked mental illness or total incompetence. For some, an old high school football injury came in handy. Sexual dysfunction of any sort worked like a charm. One gutsy way to avoid induction was to wear lace panties to your physical.

Some of the luckiest ones got into the National Guard. Now that was a very good deal. Anyone who got into the Guard could have it both ways—avoid the jungles of Vietnam and look patriotic at the same time. But who got into the Guard in those days? For the most part, only men who could pull the right strings – professional athletes or sons of the well-connected. I remember later in the war when the Boston Patriots selected running back Carl Garrett in the first round of the 1969 NFL draft. His hometown draft board in Texas also drafted him. No problem. Everyone was ready to let someone else go and possibly die in his place. The Patriots (you have to love the irony in the name) legally moved Garrett's place of residency from Texas to Massachusetts where, wonders of wonders, a spot opened in the Massachusetts National Guard. Garrett served his six months in the off season and had an even better rookie year than another famous 1st round NFL draft pick—O. J. Simpson. The system worked beautifully for Garrett. But for the son of a bricklayer who ran the 40 in an hour and a half, getting into the National Guard was harder than passing a camel through the eye of a needle.

By 1968, the unfairness of the draft system was obvious to all. So the Selective Service, the agency that administered the draft, introduced the lottery. Now young men would be drafted based on their birth date. It was hoped that this would produce an army more representative of the nation as a whole. Still, Richard Nixon didn't want to alienate middle-class voters. So he allowed student deferments to remain in place until 1971. By then the Vietnamization policy had greatly lowered the monthly draft calls. Vietnamization was a classic illustration of "what goes around comes around." We had gone back to our original position that Asian boys should fight Asian wars.

*****

Back in early 1966, however, the overwhelming sentiment was in favor of the war. On March 1, by a vote of 92 to 5, the United States Senate rejected a proposal to rescind the Gulf of Tonkin Resolution. This vote allowed Johnson to continue waging war anyway he saw fit. Even on college campuses, a clear majority of the students believed in the war, even if they weren't so keen on their own personal involvement. Most thought the fighting would be over by the time they graduated anyway, so they didn't sense any personal danger in their pro-war stance. At the time no one could have forecast that the Vietnam War would turn out to be the longest major conflict in American history.

Attitudes about the war did slowly change. In 1968, campuses would explode in violence. The Vietnam War would no longer be seen as a distant war with few consequences on the home front. In 1966, however, even the men in Vietnam were pretty naive about the war—its causes and its likely long-term consequences. Most had a sense that we were somehow engaged in a noble enterprise. So morale, overall, was good. My own morale was all over the place. On bad days I was fixated on how much I hated being in the army and how much I hated the war and what damage we were doing to the Vietnamese people. On the other hand, I grew to love Vietnam and Asia in general.

Henry Billings

My distaste for America's presence in Vietnam put me in the clear minority. Most soldiers thought we could make a difference. They believed American soldiers could make the rice paddies and villages "safe for democracy." At least for many of the analysts in the 519th, the war seemed worth fighting. After all, we had not come to conquer Vietnam; we had come to liberate it. There was something American and innocent about the way many of us viewed this conflict. Our war dead had barely topped 1,000 by the end of 1965. We had a long way to go to fill up that future black wall on the mall. Our early optimism would fade in time.

*****

There was, naturally, no one "Vietnam" experience. All of the more than 2 million men and women who served there had their own experience. But there were some broad fault lines to service in Vietnam. To be sure, the experience of Saigon warriors was light years from that of the combat soldiers. Second lieutenants in the Iron Triangle or I Corps got killed. In Saigon, the risk was, to say the least, much lower. The single worst thing that happened to me physically was field root canal by a rookie dentist. It was done in a tent by a guy who I swear would have made a good protege of Josef Mengele. The operation took three visits. I think the dentist, doing his first real root canal, wanted to drag it out. To him, it was good practice. On my last visit, he was using a tiny drill to clean out the remaining nerve ends when he crashed through the bottom of the tooth and into my gums. I must have leapt three feet out of the chair. "I don't think we're going to be able to save the tooth after all," he said then. "We'll have to pull it."

Now he wanted to practice extractions. He poked around in my mouth a little bit more. Still fractious from the needle plunge into my gums, I mumbled, "Well, pull the son-of-a-bitch."

"I already did," he said with a grin.

VIETNAM FOLLIES
A Memoir of an Intelligence Officer

Root canal aside, Colonel Gilliland insisted each of us get to the front lines to see the war first hand. I visited Ed Dandar, my old IOBC roommate, who was serving in the Mekong Delta. Like many other combat officers, Ed had a kind of boyish optimism about the future of the war. He talked endlessly about the progress he and his South Vietnamese unit were making.

The second major fault line is related to the first. Officers in Saigon got to live in the city in real homes. (Ed's room was a small hooch surrounded by sandbags.) We didn't have to live on the base or in any barracks. We could rent our own place anywhere in the city. So I went with five other guys to look around. We found a modest place just off Thuong Minh Giang, one of the main roads running from Tan Son Nhut to downtown. It wasn't anything fancy, but it was home. The place was basically two large concrete rooms, one on top of the other. The lower level front street entrance had a huge green metal door that slid open. We had a jeep but it was suicide to leave it overnight on the street. Only bad things could happen if we left it parked there. The jeep would either be stolen (the good option) or we would be blown up the next morning when we turned the ignition (the bad option). So every night we opened the green door and drove the jeep right into the living room. (A couple of months later, we lost the jeep when the senior officer among us moved out.)

Our home had a second-story balcony that overlooked an open-air market. The back of the house was open to the elements. So the house wasn't safe. Anyone could have easily slipped in from one of the neighboring homes and killed us. The possibility frightened us, and for the first couple of weeks, one of us stayed up all night on guard duty. (The army gave us each an M-14 rifle. But, perhaps fearing we might hurt ourselves, army officials gave us just one clip with 20 rounds. So there we were: armed to the teeth with three and a third bullets each.) After a cuople of weeks, we just said, "Fuck it." We all needed our sleep. And, in any event, we had no real defense against anyone who took it into his or her mind to dust us. Every kid in the neighborhood was better armed than we were.

We had to adjust to other forms of life in the house. None of us was used to life in the tropics. I, for one, had never seen a cockroach before and I had never seen the little lizards that crawled around the ceiling and walls eating malaria-bearing mosquitoes. The lizards spooked me when I first saw them. One afternoon I was lying bare-chested in bed. We had just sprayed poison everywhere to kill the cockroaches. I was beginning to doze off when I felt a thud on my chest. I opened my eyes to see this lizard staring me in the face with big blank eyes. My heart nearly stopped. I had never been so frightened in my life. The poison fumes had drifted up to the ceiling and killed him as he crawled over my bed. The poor guy fell and made a perfect four-point landing inches from my face. Not much of a war story, no Purple Heart, but there it is.

*****

We had two house servants. One was a 14-year-old boy named Ba whose basic job it was to stay in the house for security reasons while we were away. He also did some shopping and bargaining for us in the market directly across the street. We also had a young girl named Thinh. She was maybe 14 or 15. She came in a few times a week to dust and clean up. She also shined shoes and washed the sheets.

One day Thinh got the shock of her young life. She came up the stairs where one of my roommates was sleeping under a mosquito net in nothing but his underwear. Herb was a black man—a really large black man. I stood 6 feet, 3 inches and he was bigger than me. Evidently Herb was having an erotic dream of some kind. Thinh, who couldn't have been more than 4 feet, 6 inches came running down to the first floor giggling like mad. She then pulled me up the stairs to show me something. Once there she started pointing frantically with one hand while

VIETNAM FOLLIES
A Memoir of an Intelligence Officer

covering her mouth with the other. You could have run a flag up it. To her, it must have seemed like the eighth wonder of the world. Since she and I communicated mostly in sign language, I wasn't sure if she was frightened or just powerfully impressed. I had seen Herb naked before but never like that. Herb slept through the whole thing, never moving any of his other muscles.

Our accommodations were the lap of luxury compared to what the guys in the field endured. An officer friend of mine from IOBC had drawn the short straw. He, too, had wanted to be an intelligence officer. Instead, he was assigned to a rifle company as a platoon leader. Within a couple of weeks, all the other officers were killed and he became the company commander. Later, he came to Saigon on R&R. (Note that his R&R was in Saigon while guys like me got to go to Japan or Hong Kong or Bangkok.) When he saw where I lived, he wondered out loud whether we were fighting in the same war.

The third major fault line was time. By 1968, and surely after President Nixon decided to bug out under the cover of his "Vietnamization" program begun in 1969, it was a totally different war. Vietnam is now remembered for scenes of soldiers smoking dope out of the barrel of a gun and making peace signs But when I was in Vietnam the words marijuana or cocaine or heroin never crossed my lips. Not once. As far as I knew, there was no drug scene at all in Vietnam in 1966. (I had to go back to the United States to discover the drug culture.)

One of the tragic ironies of the war was that more Americans died getting out of Vietnam than getting in. We couldn't just declare victory and leave. We couldn't simply admit that we had made a mistake. Instead, our soldiers suffered through an agonizingly long withdrawal. So who can blame the soldiers at the tail end of the war for getting stoned?

By 1969, the only "noble purpose" was to cover President Richard Nixon's ass on the way out the back door. How many men died so that Nixon wouldn't be, in his words, "the first President to lose a war?" This was also the time when our soldiers began killing their own officers. No one knows for sure how many first lieutenants and captains were killed by their own men after ordering them to go on yet another pointless patrol. But it happened. Absolutely no one wanted the distinction of being the *last* American to die in Vietnam.

****

Our office was right next to the main runway. By 1966, Tan Son Nhut had become the busiest airport in the world—even busier than O'Hare in Chicago. Well over 1,000 planes a day took off or landed at Tan Son Nhut. It was impossible to look up in the sky and not see a jet plane or a helicopter. But this wasn't just a military base. It was also a commercial airport. "It's the only place I know of where a passenger can sit back sipping a martini and watch an air strike going on below," said one commercial pilot.

Every day I saw the bizarre collection of planes in the taxi lane. There were camouflaged cargo planes loaded to drop toxic chemicals to defoliate the jungle. (The catchy slogan for the pilots of these planes was "Only You Can Prevent Forests.") There were single engine spotter planes. There were Pam Am 707 jets and smaller commercial planes. And, of course, there were fighter planes. In all, thirty-nine different kinds of planes used the airport. The one thing they all had in common was that they always climbed as fast as possible once they took off. Like me, the pilots knew how easy it would be for the Viet Cong to shoot them down. They wanted to get out of range as fast as possible. They also had to make way for the plane taking off right behind them. In short, Tan Son Nhut was a madhouse.

The other great danger most of these pilots faced was each other. There was always the risk of a high-speed jet landing at 170 miles an hour and plowing over a Piper Cub poking along at 40 miles per hour. Then there was the risk of a mid-air collision as dozens of planes circled the airport waiting to land. To make matters even worse, there was another huge airport just 14 miles north of Saigon at Bien Hoa. The landing patterns for the two airports were only 5 miles apart. During times of heavy fog, pilots often became confused. On more than one occasion, a pilot would land at Tan Son Nhut under guidance from Bien Hoa and vice versa. Among the unsung heroes of this situation were the air-traffic controllers at both airports.

Even at night, fighter jets roared down the runway headed for God-knows-where to kill God-knows-who. I got a chill down my spine every time I saw the red glow from their engines arc into the night sky. We had so much raw power. It seemed incredible that the puny Viet Cong would dare defy us. We had all the planes, all the tanks, all the hi-tech gadgets. By any statistical measure, this war paired a microbe against Godzilla. Yet I often walked by a quieter part of Tan Son Nhut. That was my reality check. Next to one large hanger, a few soldiers would be stacking metal coffins with American flags draped over them. Some microbe.

Although we were comfortable in Saigon, we were still at war. So we worked seven days a week. In the Research and Analysis Branch, we had two shifts. Half of us worked the day shift—from 7 AM to 7 PM—while the other half worked the reverse. I started on nights and was switched to days halfway through my tour. Each shift had its advantages. The day shift left the nights open for trips to downtown Saigon. Although I could eat on the cheap at Tan Son Nhut, I almost always went downtown to dine. The food was a bit more expensive, but I could afford it. In addition to my regular pay, I got combat pay (no kidding), a cost-of-living allowance, and a housing allowance. And since I was serving my country, I paid no taxes. Working the night shift was no one's choice. It was almost impossible to get any decent sleep during the day. On the other hand, it did allow me to play golf at the Saigon Country Club, which was right next to the airport.

Henry Billings

    Each of us was assigned a "desk." My desk was Cambodia. Others had Laos or North Vietnam or some other specialty. My job was to read and write. All sorts of documents landed on my desk. They were all classified "confidential" or "secret" or "top secret." Nothing was left unclassified. None of us knew what information might be helpful if it fell into the wrong hands. So we didn't take any chances. In addition to reading every report on our assigned country or specialty, everyone in our office had special projects to research and write about. Two of my specialties were B-52s attacks and VC morale. I hadn't caused any trouble since I left the ship. But now my personal war with the Army was about to heat up again.

VIETNAM FOLLIES
A Memoir of an Intelligence Officer

Chapter 5 ~~ Garbage In—Garbage Out

"There are three kinds of lies: lies, damned lies, and statistics"
—Benjamin Disraeli (1804-1881)

Our job at the Research and Analysis Branch was to analyze battlefield data and captured enemy documents and try to make some sense out of what we read. To be of any use at all, the work had to be objective and truthful. The numbers coming in had to be honest if there was to be any hope that the analysis going out would be honest. Unfortunately, neither was usually the case. The numbers coming in were fraudulent and the analysis going out was worse. Anyone with even a passing interest in the Vietnam War knows how shaky the so-called "body count" numbers were. If we killed as many Viet Cong and North Vietnamese soldiers as we claimed, how come they didn't quit?

Yet high body counts, real or imagined, were absolutely essential. They were needed to show that individual commanders were doing one hell of a fine job and, more importantly, that we were winning the war. Americans, most of whom couldn't find Vietnam on a world map before 1966, had little deep interest in the war. To placate them and to keep the anti-war movement on the political fringes, it was critical that there be "a light at the end of the tunnel." We had to show that the war was being won and that it would soon be over. The war was fought by the numbers for the numbers. Victory was always just around the corner; we merely had to hang in there a little longer. Americans, as a whole, swallowed the lie. They believed their leaders. Secretary of Defense Robert McNamara certainly appeared to be speaking the truth. This tough-minded, hard-headed realist seemed to have the facts. He had the necessary charts and graphs. And according to him, the trend lines were all positive.

Henry Billings

He would assure the American people by saying such things as "every quantitative measure we have shows we're winning this war." Besides, people asked each other, didn't he once run Ford Motor Company? Who could argue with a guy so smart? Certainly few people on Capital Hill dared to do so. McNamara simply dazzled them with his brilliant mind and his apparent command of the subject. But, in truth, he didn't have a clue. He saw all the trees but the forest mystified him.

If it wasn't so tragic, it would be funny. In early March, U.S. Marines swept through an area thought to be controlled by the Viet Cong in a "Search and Destroy" operation. The Marines claimed to have killed 314 VC but, strangely, they captured only 18 weapons.

Now, in your gut, you know that no VC unit would ever be caught so poorly armed. They were much too good for that. The real answer, of course, was that the 314 KIA (killed in action) were not all VC. In fact, the majority were civilians who happened to be in the wrong place at the wrong time. But in the sick numbers game of the Vietnam War, a dead Vietnamese— any dead Vietnamese—was a dead VC.

In his 1977 book, *Dispatches,* Michael Herr wrote, "Search and Destroy, more a gestalt than a tactic, [was] brought up alive and steaming from the Command psyche. Not just a walk and a firefight, in action it should have been named the other way around, pick through the pieces and see if you could work together a count, the sponsor wasn't buying any dead civilians."

Sitting placidly in their living rooms, Americans were constantly fed phony numbers about enemy dead. Each week they learned that week's casualty numbers. TV networks dutifully reported the results passed on to them by the military as if they were football scores. Network news broadcasts used four boxes with numbers to represent American, ARVN (Army of the Republic of Vietnam), Viet Cong and North Vietnamese dead. There was never a box for civilian dead. There was never a box for dead children or women who happened to get in the way.

VIETNAM FOLLIES
A Memoir of an Intelligence Officer

Some estimates suggested American and ARVN forces were killing 10 civilians for every honest-to-God VC cadre. (On the other hand, it should be noted that most of the people in rural areas, if forced to choose sides, would have chosen the Viet Cong. So most of the "civilian" dead were at least Viet Cong sympathizers. The reason was clear. The VC fought for national independence. The same could not be said for the gangsters running the South Vietnamese government.)

There were other factors involved. Sometimes two separate units counted the same dead bodies. This "double-counting" was fairly common. Sometimes direct inspection of bodies wasn't possible because the jungles and swamps made it virtually impossible to find all the dead bodies. In that case there were dead who were not reported. Also, the Viet Cong and North Vietnamese were notably conscientious about removing their dead from the battlefield as quickly as possible. So American and ARVN commanders often had to guess how many enemies soldiers they had killed. ARVN officers were famous for guessing high. Most American commanders tried to give an honest count, but they, too, had no incentive to guess low. The end result was a KIA count that was often inflated, sometimes grossly so. The war was never going as well as the American people were led to believe.

Military intelligence officers never knew the complete truth. For them it was like trying to manage a baseball team without knowing how many runs had already been scored. In 1966, only one thing was beyond dispute. The more enemy soldiers we "killed," the stronger the enemy got. It amazed me even then that we could report killing so many of them and yet, somehow, they kept getting stronger and stronger.

In the same building with us, on the second floor, the Order of Battle (OB) people worked on enemy strength and the appearance of new units, either Viet Cong or North Vietnamese. The North Vietnamese kept infiltrating more and more men into South Vietnam. So it was easy to see why they grew in strength.

But why would VC units be getting stronger? Was there something wrong with the way we were counting the enemy? (Some analysts in the CIA felt MACV was undercounting the true strength of the VC. It was not a minor quibble. The difference in numbers ran into the hundreds of thousands.) Was it possible our indiscriminate killing was driving the people into the arms of the communists? Why were so many of them so willing to risk their lives against a superpower like the United States? What was wrong with these people anyway?

It was playfully suggested at the time that maybe it would be better to just pay off the VC. A little bribery never hurt. Give all the VC a few thousand bucks and tell them to be good from now on. It would have been a lot cheaper than the war. In 1966, some amateur mathematician figured out that it cost the United States about $350,000 for each VC we killed. Of course, if you eliminated all the people we killed who were not real VC cadre, the per dead capita rate would have been in the millions.

****

If the problem with "body count" was too many phony numbers, the problem with B-52 attacks was not enough numbers of any kind. The first report I wrote covered the initial six months of B-52 strikes against South Vietnam. Actually, I didn't write the report. I rewrote it. Another officer had tried his hand before I got there. But he hadn't done a satisfactory job. He had praised the B-52 for being the "most awesome weapon ever in the history of human warfare" or some such overblown phrase. Even the U.S. Air Force, which embraced the bomber with all its heart, couldn't approve his report. It was too far over the top even for them. My job was to praise the fine job the B-52s were doing but to couch it in more moderate tones. I wasn't supposed to redo the basic research. The first writer had already done it or had been handed a set of meager but well-cooked

VIETNAM FOLLIES
A Memoir of an Intelligence Officer

numbers. So I dutifully did my best with what I had. I rewrote the report and the Air Force liked my version.

In June of 1966, however, I got the job of writing the report yet again – this time from scratch. Turns out the earlier one had been just an interim study. The military wanted a thorough analysis. So now we had a full year of strikes to analyze and write about. This time I was free to do my own research. The earlier six-month report, entitled *The Effectiveness of B-52s*, would bare no resemblance whatsoever to what I was about to write. So far in my brief military career, I had only pissed off a few army people. I was about to piss off the Air Force.

But first, let's back up a bit. The B-52 was built as a *strategic* bomber. It flies five or six miles up in the sky over its intended target. These planes weigh 450,000 pounds and stretch 185 feet wingtip to wingtip. In other words, they are huge. The B-52 was designed to drop its payload of 500-pound and 750-pound bombs on cities like Moscow or Beijing or Hanoi or on industrial complexes and railroad centers. It was not designed to be a *tactical* aircraft. The B-52 was not supposed to provide close combat support to troops on the ground the way a helicopter or a jet fighter might. Given the unique nature of the guerrilla war in South Vietnam, we shouldn't have used *any* planes. This was a war that had to be won on the ground. But if planes were going to be used, we should have used tactical aircraft only. Think about it. The enemy held no cities. They didn't mass tanks. (In fact, the enemy didn't use *any* tanks until much later in the war. The most memorable feat of enemy tank power was their victory lap through the streets of Saigon on April 30, 1975.) They didn't live in high concentrations like, say, the Americans at Bien Hoa or Danang. So why did the United States insist on using B-52s to blow up trees in South Vietnam? Good question.

Simply put, the top brass thought the bombers did a terrific job. In November 1966, General Westmoreland wrote the commander of the 4133 Bomb Wing stationed at Anderson Air

Henry Billings

Force Base on Guam. "The effectiveness of the Arc Light (B-52 bombing) program has been proven in Vietnam as a means of breaking up large enemy formations, disrupting the enemy's supply and communications lines, penetrating other inaccessible base areas and creating a deep-seated psychological fear among the enemy."

Clearly, my report hadn't reached Westmoreland. Or if it did, he must have filed it in the trash bin. The truth was that he had little or no evidence on which to base such a claim. When I researched the data on the first year's bombings, I found almost nothing. The Air Force flew over 180 "saturation bombing" missions. Each mission included anywhere from 3 to 27 planes. We dropped many thousands of tons of bombs and blew the crap out of the dirt. Some critics called these bombing raids "matchwood missions" because they blasted trees into such little bits they were suitable only for making matches. But that's about all we did.

I checked many of the photos taken by reconnaissance planes that flew over the bombed areas. In almost every case, all I could see was a large hole in the ground. The triple-layered jungle canopy was so high and dense I couldn't see if there was any collateral damage. Once in a while there would be a big hole in a road. Westmoreland must have seen this as evidence of "disrupting the enemy's supply and communications lines." As if a hole in a road would stop such a determined enemy. North Vietnamese soldiers had spent months climbing over narrow mountain passes and hacking their way through jungles just to reach South Vietnam. A few potholes in the Ho Chi Minh Trail weren't going to stop them.

The bombs probably collapsed some VC tunnels, but we couldn't tell for sure from the photos. Even if some tunnels did cave in, the only net result was that the VC dug deeper tunnels the next time. As we later discovered, the VC were master tunnel builders. They even built hospitals and schools underground. The Cu Chi tunnel complex, now a popular tourist attraction, has

VIETNAM FOLLIES
A Memoir of an Intelligence Officer

over 124 miles of interconnected tunnels and is 23 feet deep in places. Some of the tunnels ran right under American bases. Amazingly, all the tunnels were dug by hand, without cement or any help from modern technology.

If the aerial photos showed little visible damage, I thought perhaps our guys on the ground had seen evidence of how effective B-52s were. But they hadn't. In fact, they couldn't. During the first year of bombing, there was virtually no ground follow-up operations by the infantry to any of these bombings. Westmoreland himself talked about the enemy's "inaccessible base areas." No American soldiers rushed into the bombed area to count dead bodies. In fact, the total number of confirmed dead Viet Cong or North Vietnamese KBA (killed by air) from B-52s *strategic* bombing missions over South Vietnam from June of 1965 to June of 1966 was exactly zero!

Ironically, there were six KBAs from one *tactical* support mission. A flight of B-52s gave close combat support to the First Cavalry Division's fight in the Ia Drang Valley. In this case, we had soldiers on the ground to check the damage. It struck me as weird at the time that B-52s did their best proven work doing a job they were not designed to do. Later in the war, B-52s rained down massive payloads on the industrial and populated areas of North Vietnam. Now that was *strategic* bombing! During the so-called "Christmas" bombing raids of 1972, wave after wave of B-52 bombers blasted the region between Hanoi and Haiphong, trying to force the North Vietnamese back to the bargaining table. Those bombings killed more than 1,000 people. (The number would have been much higher but the North Vietnamese evacuated most of the people before the bombs hit.)

Westmoreland was right about one thing, however. The bombings scared the shit out of the VC and any one else who happened to be in the neighborhood. I read diaries of captured enemy soldiers who wrote about their fear of unseen planes and the ground suddenly exploding around them. Some literally shit their pants. Others cried. The blasts made others temporarily deaf. No, there was no doubt that B-52s were a fear-provoking weapon. That was especially true on those occasions when the enemy was caught by surprise. A North Vietnamese soldier later reported, "The first time I was attacked [by B-52s] was in Ben Cat. We were eating in our bunkers... It was like a giant earthquake. The whole area was filled with fire and smoke. Trees were falling all around... I felt as if I were sitting in a metal case which someone was pounding on with a hammer. I was sure I was dying."

In a sense, we used the B-52 as a weapon of terror. That's certainly what Westmoreland meant when he wrote about "deep-seated psychological fear." (A 500-pound bomb dropped from 5 miles up was a highly impersonal form of terrorism. The pilots never saw the people below. VC terrorism, on the other hand, was extremely personal. They looked their victims in the face before they slit their throats.) But as I discovered, the B-52 had short-lived success even as a weapon of terror. VC diaries showed that the enemy soon learned to cope with B-52 attacks. And, in a strange way, the attacks bolstered their morale. There they were on the ground with little or no protection. Up in the sky, the world's greatest military power was using its greatest plane *and yet the VC were still hanging on!*

There were a few reasons why panic among the VC and North Vietnamese eased a bit after they experienced—and survived—a few B-52s attacks. For openers, many of the bombs missed the mark. Strategic bombing, of course, isn't meant to be precise. The goal is to saturate the target area. But even given that, 50% or more of the bombs sometimes fell outside the target area. (Better radar systems improved accuracy later in the war.)

Second, the bombers struck in a predictable pattern. Three planes would fly by and drop their bombs in the first sector. The next three planes would drop their bombs in the next sector, and so on. In short, the giant planes moved like pieces on a checkerboard, moving from one square to the next. I read captured enemy documents that instructed their men to jump into the craters left by the first wave of bombers. They had figured out that we would never hit the same exact place twice. Bomb craters became the VC's best bomb shelters.

A third reason why the enemy grew to fear the B-52 less than they should have was that they often knew when an attack was coming. The bombers flew in a straight line from Guam to their targets. Along the way, the planes passed over the South China Sea where Russian trawlers and Vietnamese fishing boats were sailing. It was a simple matter to note the time and direction of the planes and to guess the probable time and target of the attack. Also, during this early period of B-52 attacks, safety regulations forced the bombers to register their flight paths and times with international air traffic controllers located in Hong Kong. Communist agents in Hong Kong got copies and passed the information to Hanoi. The warnings were then passed to COSVN (Central Office South Vietnam) and on to the units operating along the flight path. Reducing the element of surprise mitigated somewhat the psychological terror caused by B-52s.

And lastly, it took the military several days or even a week to get a target approved by the fragmented command structure. A report would come in that a VC or North Vietnamese unit was spotted in a certain area. By the time all the layers of authority had approved the target, the VC or North Vietnamese unit had moved on. So most of the time, we were bombing old news. That, of course, is one of the neat things about traditional *strategic* targets such as cities or factories or oil refineries. They don't move. On the other hand, neither do hospitals and residential homes. During the Christmas bombing of 1972, due to a slight navigational error, we blew up Bach Mai, Hanoi's best hospital. We also destroyed homes in a residential district.

Bombing guerrillas from 30,000 feet didn't make any sense to me. But it was worse than senseless. The B-52 strikes actually hurt *our* war efforts. It galvanized the enemy. Like so many other targets of bombings, the victims emerged from the strikes with fire in their belly. Also, some innocent peasants were killed by the bombs. How many of those who survived decided to join the VC as a result of bombing raids?

So, again, why did we do it? My own theory was the U. S. Air Force wanted to join in the action. Why should the army and the Marines get all the glory? Also, we had all those bombs just sitting around in Guam. Why not drop them where they might do some good?

Then, too, B-52 flights over South Vietnam were almost completely risk-free. Not one plane was shot down. Not one crew member lost his life due to enemy action. (Eight airmen did die, however. It happened on the very first mission, on June 18, 1965. Twenty-seven B-52s took off from Guam to bomb Ben Cat 40 miles north of Saigon. Sadly, two of the planes collided, killing everyone on both planes. But this was an accident. It had nothing to do with the enemy. The same thing could have happened on a training mission.)

Pilots on strategic bombing runs faced no greater risk – prior to September 11, 2001 -- than a commercial jet pilot flying from New York to LA. For the pilots the job was a "milk run." My image of these men, admittedly unfair, was that they took off early in the morning, ate a ham sandwich along the way, maybe listened to a ball game over armed forces radio, dropped their bombs, hooked a U-turn, and were back in Guam in time for Happy Hour and an early evening softball game.

Americans back home driving "Unsafe at Any Speed" Corvairs faced more danger than these pilots. The Viet Cong simply had no weapons that might shoot B-52s down. They had no fighter planes, no ground-to-air missiles, no antiaircraft fire. So from the Air Force's point of view, why not use B-52s? There was nothing to lose. Later, over North Vietnam, there was real danger involved. Then pilots faced Soviet missiles. The North Vietnamese shot down several B-52s.

B-52 pilots, of course, were only doing their jobs. They had spent their professional lives training to bomb the Soviet Union. But now they were bombing the jungle where many innocent people lived and worked. Yes, the enemy was there, but so too were women and children. In his 1967 book *Air War – Vietnam*, Frank Harvey wrote this about B-52 pilots: "It's not a mission of their choosing. It's just the way the ball happened to bounce. But one can't help but wonder what a man thinks about, after he'd set fire to 50 square miles of jungle from high altitude with a rain of fire bombs, and wakes up in his room in the darkness – and lies awake watching the shadows on the ceiling."

****

During my research I discovered we had bombed Laos at least once during that first year of B-52 bombings. It is common knowledge now, but at the time it was top secret. In fact, it was so top secret that I had to purge it from my own top-secret report. Apparently even the military recognized that bombing a neutral country wasn't a cool thing to do. It wouldn't play well back in the States.

I found out about Laos after I had been given a map of South Vietnam with numbered circles. The circles indicated bombed areas. A circle with a "3" meant that the location had been hit by B-52s three times. I was puzzled to see that these figures didn't match the total number of aerial follow-ups. The total numbers of follow-ups was one more than the map total. "What's missing?" I asked an Air Force colonel. He told me one of the attacks had been in Laos but I couldn't mention it in my report. Two years later, I learned that even Vice President Hubert Humphrey hadn't been told about the bombing of Laos.

Humphrey's ignorance clearly illustrates one of the flaws in military intelligence reports during the Vietnam War. No one, especially officers seeking rapid advancement, wanted to be the bearer of bad news. So they put the best possible spin on everything. That's why administration officials never perceived the light at the end of the tunnel as an oncoming train. Make your boss happy and move up. Make your boss's boss happy and move up twice as fast.

As a result, the further up the line the analysis went, the more corrupt it became. Each level filtered out a bit more of the hard truth and added a splash more wishful thinking. Or, to put it another way, the war news got better and better. Under such circumstances, it was possible for a lowly second lieutenant to know more about some aspects of the war than the Vice President of the United States.

****

Finally I sat down to write my report. Obviously, I didn't care about promotion or, for that matter, pleasing my boss. I wanted to tell it like I saw it. The first thing I did was change the title. In my version, the report was no longer called *The Effectiveness of B-52s* but simply *The Effects of B-52s*. This was an honest title. I could write about "effects" because it was an absolute term and meant simply listing all the verifiable damages caused by B-52s. "Effectiveness"—a relative term—implied something that I couldn't begin to prove. These planes were not effective. The United States was spending oodles of money to level trees and terrorize whoever happened to be in the area.

In the report itself, I listed all the known damage—roads interdicted, buildings destroyed, bridges blown up, etc. To be sure, all the numbers were small. In my conclusion, I wrote that no one really knew how "effective" the bombers were. We just didn't have enough data to support any definitive claim. The best evidence we had came from the enemy. Captured diaries and enemy documents convinced me the bombings hurt us more than helped. Blowing up a country to save it wasn't such a hot idea.

Well, as you've probably already guessed, the Air Force people exploded then they saw my final draft. In long and heated discussions with top Air Force officers, I defended my findings and conclusions. We argued about my new title. (Colonel

VIETNAM FOLLIES
A Memoir of an Intelligence Officer

Gilliland, to his credit, did his best to defend me and my work.) But in the end, the report was taken out of my hands. An army second lieutenant doesn't win many battles with Air Force colonels. In the end, the Air Force basically just said, "Nice job, we'll take it from here."

As far as I know, the report vanished into the black hole of military bureaucracy. I'm not even sure it was read by Brigadier General Joseph A. McChristian, Westmoreland's chief of military intelligence in Vietnam. Or perhaps by the time it reached him it had been rewritten to offer a glowing endorsement of B-52s. In any case, my efforts had absolutely no effect on our strategy. Westmoreland's comment to the SAC commander was made just after I left Vietnam. The Air Force did recognize that there was indeed a problem. But it wasn't with the B-52. It was with B-52 reports. They stopped them cold.

As for the B-52s, the Air Force put even more bombs on them. In 1965, the average bomb tonnage per plane was 17. By 1970, the average bomb tonnage had moved up to 28. Which all goes to prove, once again, that you can never have too much of a bad thing.

By 1973, when we stopped all B-52 bombings, a total of 126,615 combat sorties had been flown over North and South Vietnam. We dropped more than 2.5 *million* tons of ordnance. That was far more than we dropped on Germany and Japan combined during World War II. And still, we lost the war.

Whatever people think about the use or misuse of the B-52, the bomber definitely made an impact on Hanoi. In January 1998, the North Vietnamese opened to the public its B-52 Victory Museum. It was designed to remind the Vietnamese people of the awesome weapons used against them. Visitors get to see the enormous size of the wheel and the immense wingspan of the B-52 bomber. Nguyen Minh Tam, the museum's director, said, "We want to show people how big these planes are." Tam went on to say the museum wasn't intended "to humiliate the

Americans. We want to remind people, especially our young people, of what we had to overcome."

The North Vietnamese even had a patriotic song about B-52s. It includes these less-than-subtle lyrics: "Our will and wisdom are a thousand times stronger than the bombs and weapons of the enemy." Not Bob Dylan, but it makes a point.

Special Forces Lieutenant Randolph Harrison, commenting on the effect one B-52 raid had on the communists, said it had been "the same as taking a beehive the size of a basketball and poking it with a stick. They were mad."

*****

The drive for "body counts" and the use of B-52s proved to me how little the generals understood the true nature of this war. We didn't learn from the mistakes the French made. Westmoreland was asked if he was studying the lessons of the French. "Why should I study the lessons of the French?" he shot back. "They haven't won a war since Napoleon."

So instead of learning from the past, we decided to repeat it. Air Force General Curtis LeMay said, "If I had enough bombs, I could win this war, because I'd blast the Vietnamese back to the Stone Age." What LeMay didn't understand was that in many ways the Vietnamese were already living in the Stone Age. Compared to what we could throw at them, their weapons were positively primitive. (Well over 50% of all American casualties came from simple booby traps and mines. Booby traps might be as simple as a sharpened stick covered with animal dung. It could cut through a boot and cause a painful infection. Mines were also homemade. The VC made them using discarded C-ration or coffee cans. They recycled explosives from some of our dud bombs. They added a trip-wire and some nails and, voila!, they had a GI killer.) No amount of bombs or artillery shells would crush these people. We had to win the Vietnamese over to our side. But that would have required a *political* strategy and we didn't have one.

****

One final word about numbers. The United States military was obsessed with quantifying the Vietnam war. We were like bank examiners checking everyone's accounts. We counted all the stars and missed the sky. This was a direct result of General Westmoreland's decision to reject a campaign of counterinsurgency. In its place, he opted for a war of attrition, featuring search-and-destroy operations, massive bombings, and high casualties on both sides. Such a war depends on numbers. Success was measured in body counts, battles won, and the percent of the countryside controlled by both sides.

Even today, apologists still argue about the final scorecard. For example, they point with pride to the fact that neither the North Vietnamese nor the VC ever beat the United States in any significant battle. "We won all the battles," they declare. They are especially irked when people say we lost the Tet Offensive. At the time, war hawk journalist Joseph Alsop reported tons of statistics showing how badly we beat the Viet Cong in Tet. Today several Internet sites list our "so-called defeat" in the Tet Offensive as one of the enduring myths of the war. The point is debatable. But it is also totally irrelevant. The Viet Cong and the North Vietnamese knew all along what they had to do to win the war. They recognized that it was first and foremost a political struggle. That's why they spent so much time telling their troops *why* they were fighting. (Our guys, in contrast, had no clue.) It wasn't about winning real estate. It wasn't about who was "king of the mountain" after a particular battle. It was about who inflicted the most political and psychological damage. The VC and North Vietnamese won those battles hands down almost every time.

Henry Billings

The VC and North Vietnamese also knew that Americans wouldn't continue to send their sons into a meat grinder indefinitely. (Even Henry Cabot Lodge came to this conclusion. In 1968, he said American public opinion could support a long war with low casualties or a short war with high casualties. But Americans would not stand for "a long drawn-out war with high casualties.") The Vietnamese had no choice. They were in it come hell or high water. Vietnam was their home and it was their cause. They didn't rotate home every 12 months. It didn't matter if they had higher casualty rates or were driven out of a particular area. They were going to keep fighting. So it was as if we kept the score but at the end of the game they walked off with scoreboard.

VIETNAM FOLLIES
A Memoir of an Intelligence Officer

Chapter 6 ~~ Mean Streets

"Yet, finally, war is always the same. It is young men dying in the fullness of their promise. It is trying to kill a man that you do not even know well enough to hate…therefore, to know war is to know that there is still madness in the world."
—President Lyndon Johnson's State of the Union Address, January 20, 1966.

When I found out I was going to Vietnam, I tried to go with an open mind. Not that I wasn't going in with a truckload of my own prejudices. But maybe, I thought, I was wrong about the war. What did I really know, anyway? There's a reason why 24-year-olds aren't allowed to run for President. I looked at my involuntary participation in the war as a chance to see the thing up close. I don't want to put too fine a point on this, but I was open to persuasion. I knew it wasn't likely, but then, going to war was a whole new experience for me.

Others changed their minds about the war. One of the closest friends I made during army training once held views similar to mine. We thought it would be neat to correspond with college students back in the States. Our plan was to tell them what this war "was really like." We both felt that our impressions would be negative. We never launched our letter-writing campaign, however. Within a few weeks of our arrival in Vietnam, my friend did a sudden 180°. A graduate of Harvard with a master's degree from Princeton, the dove-turned-hawk became a real soldier. Slowly, we drifted apart. The gap in attitudes about the war and the army became a chasm.

What I saw and learned in Vietnam didn't change my outlook. This war was bad business. I may have been naive about many things—mind-bending drugs, for instance – but I knew that much. I had studied some history and knew the litany of man's inhumanity to man. I knew about the Japanese in Nanking, the Turks in Armenia, the Germans in Russia, and so on. It was agony to be on site where I knew people were being tortured in my name.

I never saw atrocities in person. Still, I saw a fair share of documents and photos showing cruelty and degradation. It happened behind locked cell doors in Saigon and it happened on the battlefield. Some of the photos defy description. Sadists on both sides killed prisoners in the most gruesome manner imaginable. Soldiers posed for photos with the heads of dead soldiers lined up in front of them. One VC cadre was pulled apart by four tanks moving off in different directions. An oft-repeated story tells of Americans interrogating two VC suspects in a helicopter. (At least one of the Americans must have spoken some Vietnamese.) When the suspects refused to answer the questions, a crew member tossed one of the VC out the door. That was a powerful inducement to the other guy to spill his guts. After he had told the Americans all he knew, the crew said "Thanks" and tossed him out anyway.

For some of the most vicious warriors, the death of an opponent was not enough. The corpse had to be defiled, as well. The VC, for example, would cut off genitals and stuff them into a dead American's mouth. Imagine seeing that happen to a friend of yours. Perfectly sane guys, men who loved their mothers and baby sisters, went blind with rage. The sane sometimes went berserk. In Vietnam, the cycle spun out of control. My Lai was an extreme example. But it wasn't the only one. When I saw reports of atrocities, I wondered what I would do if pushed to the brink. I wanted to believe there would always be enough humanity left inside me to resist barbarism. But without a field test, I can't say how low I might have sunk.

****

VIETNAM FOLLIES
A Memoir of an Intelligence Officer

Every once in a while, the Viet Cong reminded us that even Americans in Saigon weren't safe. In March 1966, we had heard rumors that the VC were planning some sort of April Fool's Day present. They delivered on their promise. About 5 A.M. on the morning of April 1, a huge explosion woke me up. I jumped out of bed, stammering, "They just blew up the Victoria!" (The Victoria was a hotel where many American officers lived.)

Of course, I had no way of knowing what it was. The hotel was on the other side of town. It was just one of a dozen juicy American targets. So either I made a lucky guess or my sixth sense had kicked in. In any event, I was right. The VC had blown up the Victoria. The blast was so loud it could be heard all over Saigon.

I dressed quickly and ran into the street to find a pedicab. Within 20 minutes or so, I was at the Victoria. The place was a mess, with debris shattered all over the street. The nine-story hotel was virtually destroyed. So, too, were three houses on the other side of the street. Using 200 pounds of plastic explosives, the VC had sent a very clear message. Any time, any place, we can kill you.

The attack on the Victoria had begun when a VC commando unit mowed down the guards with machine gun fire and hand grenades. The commandos then rolled a small panel truck filled with explosives up to the entrance of the hotel. The blast killed three Americans and three Vietnamese. It also wounded more than 125 people. One naval officer I had met briefly the week before was taking a shower at the time. The sliding glass door shattered, leaving him with more cuts than his doctors could count.

One of the VC commandos was caught trying to escape. He leaped onto a motorbike and tried to run through a roadblock. The 30-year-old man wounded two Vietnamese policemen with a hand grenade but was knocked off his bike by two other Vietnamese officers. The explosion reminded me how lucky we were to be living in a small house on a side street. My

Henry Billings

roommates and I just weren't important enough to attack. Blowing us up wouldn't make the front page of the *New York Times* the way this blast did.

****

The fun wasn't over yet. On April 12, 1966, the United States for the first time used B-52s to bomb North Vietnam. All previous B-52 raids had been over South Vietnam or Laos. The very next day, April 13, just ten minutes after midnight, the Viet Cong attacked Tan Son Nhut airport with a massive mortar barrage. Just coincidence? No one knew for sure.

I remember the attack well. The first mortar landed in the early morning hours. I was at my desk writing a letter to the editor of the *Boston Herald-American.* My letter protested the U.S. government's threat to reclassify all college antiwar protestors I-A. Here we were supposedly fighting for freedom in Vietnam while our government was making plans to deny freedom of expression in our own land.

When the mortar attack began, I was shaken but not panicky. Besides, I was determined to finish the letter. So I shoved my typewriter under the desk and continued typing. I figured the desk provided some shelter in case the ceiling fell in. I considered running out the door to join the fray, but I wasn't armed, so that didn't seem like a very wise idea. I decided to let the people with guns deal with the VC.

After about 20 minutes, the attack ended. I ventured outside to see how bad the damage was. I should have been a lot more scared than I was. The Viet Cong had fired their mortars with pinpoint precision. One shell scored a direct hit on a Standard Oil fuel tank, causing a huge orange fireball to light up the night sky. The VC also managed to destroy twelve helicopters and nine planes and to damage many others. A direct hit killed seven GIs and a Vietnamese civilian at the 90th Replacement Depot. (The 90th had the job of greeting soldiers who had just arrived and sending them out to their units.) More than 140 personnel at the airport were injured in the attack. No shells struck our building, but they didn't miss by much. Several damaged or destroyed planes were parked less than 200 yards away.

Panic followed the attack. Americans and Vietnamese, wearing flax jackets and carrying guns, circled the perimeter of Tan Son Nhut, threatening to shoot anyone who did not cooperate fully with their orders. This threat included journalists. Ambulances shuttled between the base and the Third Field Hospital. Armed guards rode shotgun. Some fires were still burning out of control until well after sunrise. It was an unnerving experience. But not for General Westmoreland. Our cheerleader-in-chief refused to give the enemy his due. "The Viet Cong attack fell short of its objective," he announced. As if he had a clue what the objective was.

For style and degree of difficulty, I gave the VC a 9.9 The best guess was that they fired 20 to 40 rounds. With that, they killed eight men and caused millions of dollars in damage. They also showed in this first big attack on Tan Son Nhut that even the airbase with its 20,000 troops wasn't entirely safe. And, unlike the attack on the Victoria, all the Viet Cong commandos got away. The VC didn't tell me what their "objective" was, but from my box seat it sure looked like a home run. The shelling of Tan Son Nhut illustrated again that old Vietnam war bugaboo. To the top brass, the glass was always half full. They refused to see what everyone else saw going on right under their noses. They could never bring themselves to admit, "Boy, we got our ass kicked. Let's make sure it never happens again." No, this deadly, well-executed raid was declared just another VC failure.

****

As bad as things were with the VC in April, they were—in some ways—worse with our own allies. Prime Minister Nguyen Cao Ky was a peach. He loved to parade around wearing a jumpsuit and dark sunglasses with his stewardess wife dressed to match—the Ken and Barbie of Vietnam. (He walked right by me at the Bob Hope show looking every bit the lightweight.) A fighter pilot with zero political skills, Ky was "our boy" in Vietnam. On occasion, he would buzz Tan Son Nhut airport in his jet. So whenever anyone flew low over the airport, I assumed it was just the Prime Minister showing off.

If Ky had any doubts about his standing with the Americans, they were erased by the Honolulu Conference held in early February 1966. Ky flew to Hawaii to meet with President Lyndon Johnson. The President, who had arranged the meeting almost as an afterthought to deflect attention away Senator William Fulbright's hearings on the war, embraced Ky figuratively and literally. The Honolulu Conference turned into a love-in. Ky left Hawaii feeling like he had an American imprimatur to do whatever he wanted to do. For him, that meant crushing internal opposition. For me, it meant that the inmates were still running the prison.

Prime Minister Ky held power because the "directory" of ten generals who controlled the four military districts let him. They did this because Ky was acceptable to the Americans and they wanted to keep the flow of U. S. arms and other goodies headed their way. Also, Ky didn't meddle in their districts which the generals ran like Chinese warlords. But there was a problem. Earlier, Ky promised to step aside in favor of a civilian government. Naturally, he didn't think that up on his own. He did this under U. S. pressure. The Johnson administration knew that a civilian government would look better for public opinion than a military dictatorship. But, after Honolulu, Ky backed off. Instead of handing over power, he grabbed for more. He dismissed General Hguyen Chanh Thi, who controlled the First Corps District, which included Danang. That infuriated the Buddhists who were allied with Thi and who wanted a civilian government. This move triggered domestic unrest that would last until early June.

VIETNAM FOLLIES
A Memoir of an Intelligence Officer

For about three months, Vietnam was wracked by a war within a war. I was too busy at work to follow closely the ebb and flow of Vietnamese politics. (Even one top cabinet official confessed ignorance. "I am not sure I understand myself what this turmoil…is all about.") But we all understood the critical paradox of dealing with a puppet government like Ky's. We had to control Ky while pretending we were not interfering with the internal politics of Vietnam. It wasn't easy. How can you control the puppet without looking like you're pulling the strings? It was a Zen riddle. Can a puppet with no strings dance?

Nguyen Cao Ky was no fool. He knew the game. He knew he couldn't appear to be a lackey of the Americans to his own people. Unfortunately, the Honolulu Conference left many Vietnamese thinking exactly that—Ky was an American toady. In a move to support Ky, Ambassador Henry Cabot Lodge let him borrow U. S. Air Force planes to carry his troops to "liberate" Danang which had, according to Ky, fallen into "communist hands." Such nonsense. Danang was controlled by Thi and the Buddhists. Also, there was a huge contingent of Americans stationed there. In a show of defiance, General Thi's troops blocked the road into town, forcing a standoff. Not knowing what to do, Ky backed down.

The fiasco showed how much the Americans had helped Ky. This, in turn, led to an explosion of anti-American feeling among the people of Vietnam who were *supposed to be our friends*. So now we were getting it from both sides. It made more than one American wonder what we were doing risking our lives fighting the communists to save people who not only were fighting each other but hated our guts as well.

From the time we first slipped into Saigon under the cover of darkness until I left Vietnam, I never once felt like the ordinary people of Vietnam really wanted us there. They believed that there were five evils in the world: fire, flood, famine, robbery, and the central government. With the exception of flood (we never did bomb the dikes), a case can be made that the United States was guilty of promoting all of them.

The situation was ripe for an explosion. It came right on cue. Young Vietnamese toughs, called "cowboys," filled the streets of Saigon. Night after night they roamed the streets looking for trouble. They waited for the slightest pretext to attack anything in their path. They tipped over cars, broke windows, ripped down signs, and burned buildings. They shouted anti-American and anti-Ky slogans. "Da dao [down with] Ky" and "Da dao American imperialists." It was their form of evening entertainment. For an American GI, the Saigon of 1966 was about as far away from the Paris of 1944 as you could get. Speaking of World War II images, the Buddhists called Ky a "Nazi." I tried to keep a low profile during these tense times. At night I always went from Point A directly to Point B without exploring any of Saigon's back alleys, something I ordinarily loved to do.

Rioters attacked some Americans on sight. In one reported case, a group of youths manhandled an American civilian engineer who passed by on a motorcycle with his Vietnamese girlfriend. The American, of course, was clearly asking for it. He must have been new to Vietnam. We all quickly learned the unwritten law that an American was never to be seen at night in the company of a Vietnamese female unless it was inside a bar. If this fellow wanted to be with his girlfriend for the night, fine. But the two of them couldn't ride through downtown together. They had to take separate transportation to his place. Such a breach of etiquette was bad enough when things were relatively peaceful. But when Saigon was in chaos, well, he was lucky they only burned his bike.

Rioters also attacked a dozen or so other Americans in and out of uniform. Rioters carried banners with such catchy slogans as: "Down With U. S. Obstruction," "Stop Interfering With the Vietnamese People's Aspirations," and "End Foreign Domination of our Country." Saigon became a dangerous place to be out walking the streets even during the day. Buddhists monks also joined in the marches. (For the most part, the Buddhists had no real political agenda except to end foreign domination of Vietnam and to stop the slow destruction of traditional Vietnamese values.) I can remember lying spread-eagled on our second story balcony as some Buddhist monks stretched barbed wire across Thuong Minh Giang to stop all traffic. My rifle had no bullets. One of my roommates had the clip with the 20 rounds. Still, we needed to look serious—ready to meet violence with violence. My roommates and I never fired a shot, but there were plenty of people on the street getting clubbed over the head after troops loyal to Ky came with tear gas to break up the demonstration.

Such random violence continued for weeks. No one, not even the Americans, knew what Prime Minister Ky would do next. At times, he seemed to back off. In one moment, he would hold out the hope of free elections. Then, fearing he might look weak, he would reverse himself. In early May, he again sent troops to Danang. This time fighting broke out. Ky's men killed hundreds of rebel solders. A short time later, they crushed the resistance movement in Hue as well. With friends like this, who needed the Communists?

Meanwhile, the Buddhists continued their protests. Some went on hunger strikes. Others held parades. Still others set themselves on fire. In fact, more died by immolation during this period than died that way during the struggle to topple Diem. But in the end, it was all for nothing. The generals made a separate deal with Ky and the Buddhist uprising fizzled out.

Meanwhile, the Johnson administration wasn't about to change horses in mid-stream. So the word went out that we backed Ky. He might be a son of a bitch, but he was our son of a bitch. Or in one of Johnson's more salty phrases, "It better to have him inside the tent pissing out than outside the tent pissing in."

Henry Billings

Still, real damage had been done and everyone knew it. Under American guidance, Ky launched a public relations campaign to win back some of the popular appeal. He didn't line up his enemies against a wall and mow them down. He let General Thi go to the United States. Ky also allowed the monks to stay in their temples. "Our boy" also staged musical shows and handed out candy to children.

To the Johnson administration, the whole bloody episode had been a political nightmare. Internecine warfare and burning monks didn't help the pro-war cause back home. Clearly, Ky couldn't be trusted with a free hand. So his strings had to be shortened. As for the war against the Communists—we would handle that from now on. Nguyen Cao Ky's attacks on his own people had given us one last chance to cut our loses and bug out. We didn't take it, and so America sank deeper into the Vietnamese quagmire.

VIETNAM FOLLIES
A Memoir of an Intelligence Officer

Chapter 7 ~~ Murder—Saigon Style

> *"I want to tell you, I don't think the whole of Southeast Asia, as related to the present and future safety of the people of this country, is worth the life or limb of a single American."*
> —David M. Shoup, Marine corps commandant in a May 14, 1966 speech in Los Angeles

Prime Minister Nguyen Cao Ky needed a scapegoat for Saigon's rampant corruption. Like Claude Rains in *Casablanca,* Ky was shocked, shocked that people were actually making money on the black market. An example had to be set. Ky could, of course, have rounded up the usual suspects. They weren't hard to find. They were all over the place. The government of South Vietnam and the South Vietnamese army were full of them. Anyone who held a position of power or influence in Saigon in those days was corrupt on some level. Still, Ky had to find someone to blame. He had to find someone with no political support. And he had to find someone who would provoke no widespread public sympathy.

Ky settled on a 35-year-old Chinese merchant named Ta Vinh. The Vietnamese had a long history of distrusting the Chinese. The Chinese were for the most part middle-class businessmen and bankers. (Most lived in a separate section of Saigon called Cholon.) So Ta Vinh, who ran an import-export company, was a convenient target. Ky had promised a series of anti-corruption trials to clean up the city. But this turned out to be the only trial. Everyone in Saigon knew that Ky's anti-corruption drive was nothing but a sham. Ta Vinh was quickly found guilty of profiteering, black market transactions in currency, hoarding, and attempting to bribe government officials.

Henry Billings

In reality, all of these "crimes" were a normal part of business transactions in Saigon. Every merchant operated outside the law but with the tacit approval of the government. With inflation soaring into the triple digits, no one could make a profit at the legal government price, which hadn't been adjusted for a long time. Said one source quoted in *The New York Times,* "Everybody's a bit of a Ta Vinh... Everyone would try to bribe a policeman who tried to arrest him. It's been that way for a long time."

The trial began on the morning of March 7 and ended that evening. Three Vietnamese army officers sentenced Ta Vinh to death by firing squad. A photo taken immediately after the sentencing showed a tearful Ta Vinh holding his one-year-old son. The poor man had 24 hours to appeal to Head of State Nguyen Van Thieu (who would later replace Ky as South Vietnam's most visible leader). Ta Vinh found no mercy in that quarter. His execution was initially set for early in the morning of March 13. But that was a Sunday and Ky didn't want to offend Catholics on their holy day. The execution was put off for a day.

The execution was well-publicized. That was the point—to let everyone know just how serious Ky was about weeding out corruption. He wanted an audience. Ta Vinh was to be shot in the Central Market. There was plenty of standing room for anyone who wanted to see it. Some of my friends wanted to go. They had never seen anyone executed. Hell, none of us had ever seen anyone killed. I took a pass. Watching another man, guilty or innocent, die wasn't my cup of tea. When I heard what happened, I didn't regret my decision. Journalist Stanley Karnow, who witnessed it, later wrote in his 1983 bestseller *Vietnam: A History* that he was "appalled" and declared that the execution "still sears my memory."

Ten military policemen made up the firing squad. They assembled a little after 5 a.m. It was still dark with only a hint of the approaching sunrise. Ta Vinh was tied to a stake with his hands behind him. A Catholic priest read this Buddhist his last rites. Then the condemned prisoner was blindfolded. Although Ky wanted to make a statement for domestic consumption, he didn't want photographs in the world press. So just before the order to fire was given, soldiers jumped into a series of jeeps and trucks arranged in a semicircle in front of the stake. They then raced their engines and flashed their headlights on high beam. This was done in the hopes of spoiling any pictures that might be taken. At the command of "Fire," ten shots rang out. Following that, the leader of the firing squad that walked up to the dead man and fired one additional round into Ta Vinh's head.

Throughout the ordeal, Ta Vinh's wife and his eight children, all wearing white mourning clothes, stood less than a block away. The police wouldn't let them get any closer. The wife and kids weren't even allowed to say goodbye. Even so, their cries could be heard across the market. Some U. S. officials, to their credit, tried to stop the execution. They pleaded in private and in vain. In the end, one man lay dead but corruption in Saigon simply expanded as if nothing had happened. Ky's anti-corruption campaign faded away with the echoes of the firing squad. The execution spooked the Chinese community, however. For several days afterward, trading in Cholon stopped almost completely. Some Chinese merchants sold all their stocks and took an unscheduled vacation to Hong Kong.

****

Sergeant George David Birdsell wasn't a warrior—even by Saigon standards. A 16-year veteran of the United States Army, Sergeant Birdsell was our office secretary. He was assigned to us through the 1st Logistics Command. A bit on the heavy side and out of shape, Birdsell's year in Vietnam was to be his one combat tour before he retired.

Henry Billings

A pleasant, very likeable man, Sergeant Birdsell made sure our operation ran smoothly. He was the Radar O'Reilly of our office. He knew where all the documents were and if we needed something out of the ordinary he could usually find it. As the only regular enlisted man in the Research and Analysis Branch, he didn't socialize much with the rest of us. First, he was a lot older than we were. Also, the military protocol discouraged it. Officers and enlisted men weren't supposed to pal around during off hours.

Still, Sergeant Birdsell and I shared a love of baseball; we checked the scores every day in the *Stars and Stripes*. We bet $50 on the 1966 season results. His favorite team was the Chicago Cubs and mine was the Boston Red Sox. (I had initially stuck with the Braves after they moved to Milwaukee in 1953. Slowly, however, I had begun pulling for the Red Sox. When the Braves moved once more to Atlanta, I gave up on them, though Hank Aaron did remain my favorite player.) We wagered on which of our two teams would end up with the better winning percentage for the whole year. It wasn't likely to be high in either case, since both teams sucked. We often joked about routing for such perennial losers. The last time the Chicago Cubs had won the World Series, Teddy Roosevelt was President and the last time the Boston Red Sox had won it, Adolf Hitler was still a corporal in the Austrian army. In 1966, I won the bet – the Red Sox sucked a little less than the Cubs. But, sadly, I never collected.

On June 16, Sergeant Birdsell was the duty sergeant at a compound on the outskirts of Saigon. The compound housed maybe 200 soldiers or so on temporary duty. Most were waiting to be transferred to a new unit. The compound was surrounded by barbed wire and had several towers manned by machine guns. Guards patrolled the perimeter and checked personnel as they came in and out of the entrance gate. In short, the place was fairly well-guarded against outside attacks.

VIETNAM FOLLIES
A Memoir of an Intelligence Officer

On this particular night, Sergeant Birdsell was second in command to the duty officer. Sometime after 10 o'clock, he was standing at the entrance gate that opened onto the dirt road leading to downtown Saigon. A soldier came up to him. This soldier had just recently been reassigned from his unit in the Mekong Delta for some sort of emotional problem. He had been drinking. (That, of course, wasn't unusual. Whenever we had the chance, we all drank—often to excess.) The soldier said to Sergeant Birdsell, "I'm going into town."

"I'm sorry," Sergeant Birdsell told him. "There's an 11 o'clock curfew. It's too late. By the time you get to town the curfew will be in effect. I can't let you go."

The soldier stormed off, shouting back at Sergeant Birdsell that he would talk to the duty officer. But the duty officer refused to override Sergeant Birdsell. Instead, the duty officer told this soldier the same thing. He couldn't go into town. It was simply too late. He could try again tomorrow.

At this point, something must have snapped in this young soldier's head. He returned to his bunk and grabbed his M-16. He then walked up to Sergeant Birdsell and demanded that he open the gate. Sergeant Birdsell stood his ground. The two men argued briefly and then the soldier turned the rifle on Sergeant Birdsell. He opened fire from just a few feet away. Sergeant Birdsell never had a chance. He died instantly.

Tower guards then shot the soldier, badly wounding him. I never heard what happened to this man, other than that he survived the shooting and was arrested for murder. But the only person any of us cared about was Sergeant Birdsell.

I didn't learn about his death until early the next morning when I reported to work. At first, being given no details of the murder, my mind swam with questions. How could it happen? Who had done it? My immediate assumption was that the Viet Cong had attacked the compound. It was a natural target with so many men in such tight quarters. When I heard what had really happened, I couldn't believe it.

Henry Billings

It would have been one thing for Sergeant Birdsell to die in the line of duty fighting off an enemy attack. Even a non-violent type like myself could recognize the nobility of laying down one's life to save others. But to die at the hands of a nut case who wanted to party was really tough to swallow. It seemed such a waste.

It goes without saying that Sergeant Birdsell's murder was a totally unexpected blow to all of us—like a freak car accident. It came out of the blue. No one saw it coming. How could such a thing possibly happen? Guys in our office weren't supposed to get killed and certainly not like that. But there it was, like a swift, sharp kick to the nuts. This gentle man was just doing his job. He left behind left a wife and four children. The army reported his death as the result of "non-hostile" action. Talk about an oxymoron.

Later in the war, the killing of Americans by Americans would become a scandal. We dropped napalm on each other and called it "friendly fire." And, starting around 1969, we began to "frag" officers and NCOs we didn't like for one reason or another. It seems almost certain that Sergeant Birdsell was the first American soldier to be deliberately killed by an American.

In 1969 or later, the murder might have been reported as yet another reason why the war was a mistake. But this was 1966. It was simply not the same war then. In terms of the realities of the Vietnam war, we were still in the age of innocence. The overwhelming majority of Americans supported the effort or, at least, didn't actively oppose it. People wanted to believe that we were doing something good. Bad news, especially this kind of bad news, might have shattered the dreamland most Americans were living in concerning this war. Like Nguyen Cao Ky circling his jeeps, we turned our headlights on high beam so no one could see.

*****

VIETNAM FOLLIES
A Memoir of an Intelligence Officer

As a postscript to this story, one week later, I drew the short straw and was assigned to be duty officer at the compound. I got the job because I had just been promoted from 2nd lieutenant to 1st lieutenant. The duty officer was always either a 1st lieutenant or a captain. With all the men at those ranks in Saigon, you pulled duty officer only once every few months. Luckily, I did it just once. But that was enough.

The army believed it had to do something about the murder of Sergeant Birdsell. It wasn't enough to put his killer away. So the brass decided to punish the innocent as well. As a form of group punishment, some unknown officer with too much time on his hands declared that the compound would be alcohol-free for one week. Personally, I didn't think it was a good idea to turn off the sauce. It seemed to me to be an open invitation for more violence, not less. Most of the men drank in moderation. They spent their time writing letters home or playing games in the bar. They didn't shoot each other. Of course, there were always a few harmless drunks who had to be put to bed for their own good. But now, with the absolute ban on drinking, all the men had a real grievance. They thought that they were being unjustly punished for the actions of one man.

The night I served as duty officer just happened to be the night the army turned the tap back on. Lucky me. I strapped on my .45, made a tour of the facilities, and checked for VC hiding behind the bar. The guys were drinking hard, as if trying to make up for the lost week. Still, there didn't appear to be any problems. Around midnight, I made one last inspection and then went back to the small room assigned to the duty officer. The bar was now closed and everyone was supposed to be back in his bunk.

A few minutes later, a black soldier knocked on the door. He was ripping mad because a white soldier had just thrown up on his footlocker. Now he wanted to know what I was going to do about it. I strapped my .45 back on and followed the soldier to the barracks. I had no idea what I was "going to do about it." All the men—blacks and whites—slept in one huge open room. Was I walking into the middle of a burgeoning race war? I kept thinking of what had happened to Sergeant Birdsell.

All the men I was about to face were armed and at least some were drunk. With the black soldier leading the way, I made it to his bunk, my hand resting on the handle of my gun. Sure enough, someone had thrown up on his footlocker. As I looked around, I saw a hundred pairs of eyes on me. There were voices, too, but I couldn't make out what they were saying. All I knew was that it wasn't friendly chitchat. My mind raced as I contemplated my next move. I couldn't simply ask who had done the vomiting. I knew that was a non-starter. No one was about to confess. I couldn't clean it up myself – even I was too much of an officer for that. But I couldn't ignore it. The black guy who had reported it would never let me get away with that.

Then I noticed a white kid sitting on the edge of his bed. He looked a bit shaky, perhaps even queasy. Could he be the culprit? I didn't really know, but by then I didn't care. I had to take some sort of definitive action, and fast. I needed to pin the responsibility on someone before tempers got any hotter. So I forced myself to put on a tough-guy face and walked over to the pasty white guy. I grabbed him by the collar and lifted him off the bed. Holding him just inches from my face, I shouted, "You better clean up your mess, soldier!" I went on to tell him he was a disgrace to himself, to his fellow soldiers, and to the entire United States of America. In one small part of my mind, I was watching myself in amazement as I ranted on like some sort of General Patton. (If I had gloves maybe I would have slapped him like Patton.) Mostly, though, I was just scared.

In any case, my bluff worked. Some of the white kid's friends rushed over and told me not to worry, sir, they would clean up the whole mess. "You'd better," I said sternly. "Because I'll be back to check on you."

With that, I walked slowly to the door. Outside, I picked up the pace and walked back to my room as fast as I could while

VIETNAM FOLLIES
A Memoir of an Intelligence Officer

still maintaining an officer-like posture. By the time I reached my room, I felt what little courage I had left circling the drain. Needless to say, I didn't go back to check that night. I did, however, check the next morning while the men were at breakfast. To my immense relief, the footlocker was wiped clean. In my two plus years as an army officer, that night at the compound was the closest I came to actually being one.

Henry Billings

Chapter 8 ~~ The Mouse That Roared

"From the French, Chinese and Vietnamese points of view, [Cambodians] are indifferent farmers, incapable traders, uninspired fishermen, unreliable laborers...they cannot be counted on to act in any positive way for the benefit of U. S. aims and policies."
"Psychological Operations—Cambodia"
A Pentagon study published in 1959

B-52s were not my only area of responsibility. As I mentioned before, I was the head of Cambodian desk, as well. "Head" might be putting too fine a point on it. I was the only one at the desk. I had some chiefs above me but no Indians below. I was a one-man operation. When I began, I knew almost nothing about Cambodia. So for the first few weeks, I read everything I could get my hands on about the history and culture of Cambodia and the track record of its mercurial head of state, Prince Norodom Sihanouk. He had become king in 1941 at the age of 18, but had given up the crown to his father in 1955. He did it not to give up royal power but to gain more power in the world of politics. Sihanouk walked both sides of the street. He was prince and politician.

Everyone in my Research & Analysis Branch office referred to him simply as "Snookie." We called him that from the safety of South Vietnam. Few people in Cambodia would have dared refer to him publicly in anything but the most reverential tones. The notoriously thin-skinned prince fumed if someone made light of him or his country. Sihanouk's massive ego wouldn't allow it. He was, in his own mind at least, the "father" of his country. He once described the impact of an insult on his person. "The truth is that five million Khmers (ethnic Cambodians) identify themselves totally with me. To insult me, to wound me, to humiliate me, is to strike at the Cambodian nation."

Apparently no one told Secretary of State John Foster Dulles about this quirk in Sihanouk's personality. If someone did, he obviously ignored the advice. Dulles directly insulted the prince and soured Cambodian-American relations for years to come. It happened in 1953. Sihanouk had flown to Paris to in an attempt to gain independence for Cambodia. (At that time, France ran Cambodia as a protectorate the same way it ran Annan and Tonkin, the northern two-thirds of Vietnam. The southern one-third, called Cochin-China, was a full-blown colony.) Sihanouk had no luck with the French. So he flew to the United States to plead his case with us. He fared no better in Washington D.C. But Dulles didn't leave bad enough alone. A free and independent Cambodia, he scolded the prince, was out of the question. How could the French defeat the communists in Vietnam if Sihanouk caused trouble for them? Sihanouk was playing right into the hands of the communists, Dulles said. (Dulles rejected Sihanouk's notion that French control was feeding communist support in all of French Indochina.) Also, Dulles warned, if the communists won in Vietnam, Cambodia would be next and there would be nothing Sihanouk could do to stop them.

The suggestion that Cambodia was a helpless domino without French military aid appalled the proud prince. But Dulles didn't stop there. He managed to insult Sihanouk on a personal level as well. Sihanouk had hoped to dine with President Eisenhower while he was in the States. As Ike's Secretary of State, Dulles had the final word on such matters. No invitation came. Dulles reassured Sihanouk that his trip to Washington needn't be a total waste. The secretary of state suggested that the prince take in the circus while he was in town. Dulles couldn't have degraded Sihanouk more if he had simply given him a dime, patted him on the head, and told him to go buy an ice cream.

Henry Billings

In the end, Sihanouk's lobbying efforts weren't wasted on France. Before long, the French gave Cambodia its independence and the prince, justifiably, claimed the credit. At the time, France was too busy with Vietnam to worry about a small nation with barely 6 million people. The United States, meanwhile, was finding ever more creative ways to irritate the prince. After the Geneva Accords in 1954, we sent Robert McClintock to be our first ambassador to the newly-independent Cambodia. The post was a disappointment to McClintock. He had hoped for something better—a more important country. So McClintock treated Sihanouk with great disdain. He often wore shorts and brought his dog to the palace. He lectured him constantly on the best way to handle the communists. McClintock, of course, wasn't alone in his contempt for Sihanouk. American officials in general felt that Sihanouk was hopelessly naive about the true dangers of communism aggression.

*****

One of the reasons for Sihanouk's prickliness stemmed from the fact that Cambodia had once been a truly great empire. The famous ruins of Angkor Wat testify to the magnificent glory that existed 1,000 years earlier. The good times ended after the 13th century and Cambodia slowly lost its power. Slowly, the Thais moved in from the west and the Vietnamese moved in from the east. By the middle of the 19th century, it looked as if Cambodia might cease to exist. In 1863, King Norodom I asked the French for help. France forced the Thais to return some of the lands they had taken over the years from the Cambodians.

Less than a century later Cambodia was free once more. But now it was like the Poland of Southeast Asia—a skinny 90-pound weakling that no amount of independence could cure. The sand-kicking Thais and South Vietnamese continued to squeeze Cambodia like a ripe pimple. So what could Sihanouk do to save his country? Where could he turn for help?

VIETNAM FOLLIES
A Memoir of an Intelligence Officer

Cambodia was not a member of the Southeast Asian Treaty Organization (SEATO). It was a protocol state, however, and as such it received some military aid from the United States. But that wasn't enough to woo Sihanouk. During the late 1950's and early 1960's, Sihanouk had grown increasingly suspicious about American motives. He charged that we supported the Khmer Serei, an insurgent group that opposed the monarchy. Just how much of a threat this group posed was debatable. Sihanouk, however, didn't take any chances. It was later alleged that Sihanouk executed as many as 1,000 Khmer Serei suspects during his rule. The prince also felt certain the CIA was trying to get rid of him. I wouldn't have put it past the CIA, but if eliminating Sihanouk was their goal, they did a lousy job.

In any case, Sihanouk eventually settled on a neutralist position. This policy declared that Cambodia would abstain from military or ideological alliances. In 1963, he said 'thanks, but no thanks' to U. S. aid and canceled both military and economic aid. He turned to Communist China for help. Sihanouk became an anti-American, pro-Chinese neutral. But it wasn't safe to stick any label on him. He was too slippery for that. One minute he was a friend, the next, an enemy. This was true in foreign affairs as well as domestic affairs. Like a feather floating in a storm, it was impossible to predict which way he would turn next.

On May 3, 1965, Sihanouk officially terminated relations with the United States. He said that although the United States had supported him after independence with economic as well as military aid, this aid had come with too many strings attached. We had stipulated that the weapons we gave him could only be used against Cambodian communists, not in border clashes with his real enemies at the time—the Thais and Vietnamese. We had done this because Thailand and South Vietnam were American allies. We weren't going to strong-arm our friends for the sake of Cambodia. The economic aid didn't work out so well, either. One major project was the Khmer-American Friendship Highway, which ran from Phnom Penh to Sihanoukville on the

Gulf of Siam. The road was an engineering nightmare. Potholes and washouts rendered parts of the road unusable for anything smaller than a tank. (Many years later I drove down the old Friendship Highway with some members of the U.S. mission staff and we had to use a jacked-up SUV to make the trip. A car would have disappeared into a pothole, never to be seen again.)

*****

In the official American hierarchy of lowlifes, only one species ranked lowered than the communists. At the very bottom were the "neutralists." In the American view of things, of course, a neutralist couldn't exist. The either/or politics of the Cold War demanded that someone was either with us or against us. No fence-sitting allowed. The countries that tried it—most prominently, Egypt and India – drew the wrath of the State Department.

So when I picked up the ball in early 1966, the line in the sand had been drawn. Sihanouk was considered one of the world's bad guys. Still, I liked him. I didn't mind neutralists – in fact, I considered myself to be one, at least sort of. Both Snookie and I wanted to be left alone to do our own thing. (I only slowly came to realize that his "thing" was never as benign as mine but, on the other hand, his task was a bit more formidable than mine.) In any case, I found myself rooting for him. I wanted him to survive. In 1966, Sihanouk continued to walk the tightrope of neutralism. In fact, media profiles of him were often titled, "Man on a Tightrope." It seemed to me that despite his egotism, he was only doing what was best for his country in an impossible situation.

The Cambodians and the Vietnamese have always hated each other. Although neighbors, they have vastly different cultures. Vietnam was a product of China's civilization while Cambodia was a product of India's civilization. Cambodians looked at the Vietnamese as "barbarians." The Vietnamese returned the favor and tried to wipe out Cambodian culture in lands they occupied. (The main street adjacent to the one I lived on—Thuong Minh Giang—was named for a 19th century Vietnamese general who said of the Cambodians, "Hundreds of knives should be used against them, to chop them up, to dismember them.")

Add to that centuries of bloody border conflict and wasn't hard to see why Sihanouk feared the idea of a united Vietnam. In a sense, then, a divided Vietnam was his best bet for the future. Logically, Sihanouk should have been hoping an American victory. Then Vietnam would have been permanently divided between the communist north and the non-communist south. This deep-seated contradiction plus his thin skin kept him from making a firm commitment to one side or the other. Sihanouk made my life as a so-called specialist on Cambodia tough because I never felt like I was on firm ground in making assessments about his intentions.

For example, despite his deep hatred for the Vietnamese, he helped the Viet Cong and the North Vietnamese *directly.* In 1966, he secretly agreed to let China and the Soviet Union ship military supplies to VC and North Vietnamese sanctuaries located on his side of the border. I had heard rumors about this but nothing concrete. Or maybe I didn't look hard enough, letting my pro-Snookie prejudice blind my judgment. But the truth was that his own army helped to move the goods. The irony for us was that the weapons were hauled in trucks supplied as part of the American aid program over the Khmer-American Friendship Highway.

*****

In some ways, Sihanouk was a masterful politician. He certainly pushed the right buttons to gain independence from the French. But, in other ways, he was dreadful. His domestic policy was based on 'me, me, me.' He was, after all, a prince. He believed he could do whatever he wanted to do. As we said in the army, rank has its privileges. And he had thoroughly convinced himself that what was good for him must be good for Cambodia.

Sihanouk's popularity with the people of Cambodia began to fade in 1966, however. The people suffered from high unemployment. The well-educated were especially hard hit. New tax laws, border violence, and army corruption forced many peasants to flee the country for Phnom Penh. There they saw the vast difference between the rich and the poor. It was as if the blinders had been removed from their eyes. In their rural villages they hadn't known any better. Everyone had been in the same boat. But now they lifted their faces out of the mud and saw their world in a new light. Many didn't like the view.

A year earlier, Sihanouk had found a new enemy. His name was Peter O'Toole. He had just filmed the hit movie *Lord Jim* in Cambodia. A film magazine writer asked O'Toole what he thought about Cambodia. The British actor didn't hide his feelings. He hated Cambodia, the heat, the humidity, the bugs, and the culture. He called Cambodia a primitive state. Of course, when Sihanouk got wind of O'Toole's comment, he exploded. In response, he decided to make his own movies showing Cambodia's true grandeur and beauty. When I first read about the film-making prince, I thought it was pretty cool. Make film, not war. Sihanouk was my kind of guy. Boy, was I wrong.

Sihanouk had always been fascinated by movies. But now he became obsessed. Between 1966 and 1969, he made nine full-length feature movies. He wrote, produced, and directed all of them. For actors, he picked mostly members of his own family and close friends. He and his wife, Monique, starred in some. Sihanouk picked the most heroic roles for himself. If Nero played his fiddle while Rome burned, Sihanouk was adjusting the lights and making sure the actors hit their marks while Cambodia crumbled. The vast amount of time he spent on the reel world couldn't be spent on the real world.

VIETNAM FOLLIES
A Memoir of an Intelligence Officer

Sihanouk's film-making was not, as he later called it, a harmless diversion. It had very real political consequences. He used most of his army's helicopters for his first film *Aspara*. No one dared to tell him that the choppers were urgently needed to evacuate wounded soldiers from a border clash with Thailand. Apparently, the soldiers didn't count. It was far more important to the nation that the film, glorifying Cambodia's past, be made.

Aspara won high praise within Sihanouk's circle of friends. Everyone else laughed at it. The film showed a Cambodia that existed only in Sihanouk's mind. It was his Disneyland version of reality. There was no dirt or disease. There were no barefooted cyclo drivers. Life was one long parade and everyone lived in shiny villas. Sihanouk was so pleased with himself that he continued to drain the country's limited resources to make eight more movies.

*****

In between takes, Sihanouk had a country to run. And, to be fair, he did continue to work with international leaders to insure Cambodia's territorial integrity and future well-being. During the summer of 1966, he even won some limited praise from the United States. Secretary of State Dean Rusk said that Sihanouk had "done a very constructive and positive job in the development of his own country" despite living in "an area which is in flames." For his part, Sihanouk was willing to look a bit more favorably on the United States. Perhaps, he thought, the Americans would not lose in South Vietnam. Also, the Cultural Revolution in China cast doubts on how much help he could expect from Peking.

Sihanouk went so far as to invite President Johnson's special envoy, W. Averell Harriman, to visit Cambodia. It really looked as if relations between the two countries were on the upswing. But it was not to be. On July 31, American jets bombed the village of Thlok Trach on the border between Cambodia and

South Vietnam. Several people were killed in the attack. Two days later, American jets again hit the village. This time, however, there was a team of inspectors from the International Control Commission on the scene. They were there to investigate Sihanouk's claim that the village was *Cambodian* and not Vietnamese.

When officials in Washington heard about Sihanouk's protest, they said that they had checked the maps they had on hand. The maps showed the village to be in South Vietnam. So, instead of checking *all* the maps of the area, they immediately denied Sihanouk's claim. The village was in South Vietnam, end of story. I was made aware of the bombing soon after the fact. I, too, looked at my army map. What I found was that the village was in an area where the border was clearly marked "indefinite." (Border lines had never been drawn to the acceptance of both countries. The exact border had always been in dispute.)

For several days, the United States maintained Thlok Trach was in South Vietnam. I knew that was wrong. At least, it was highly misleading. No one in the office was much interested in my view. Cambodia was my problem, not theirs. Colonel Gilliland sided with the officials in Washington. So I took it upon myself to tell the people at the American Embassy in Saigon that we might be wrong about the village. I didn't, however, use the chain of command – never my strong suit—and Gilliland blew a gasket He was justly furious that I had gone over his head. It made him look bad – as if he couldn't control his subordinates. The issue now wasn't the bombing of a neutral village, but my indiscretion. I remember it being pretty chilly around the office for the next few weeks.

As it turned out, Sihanouk was right about the village. It was thoroughly Cambodian. Everyone who lived in the tiny village was Cambodian. The ICO team confirmed it. In the end, the United States admitted the mistake and apologized for the loss of life. But it was too late. The bombing destroyed any hope that Cambodia and the United States would resume diplomatic relations. Sihanouk called off the visit by Harriman. "In order for these talks to be held," Sihanouk said, "the United States must first recognize that Cambodia is a country that has a border."

The Harriman mission, it seemed to me, had been our last best hope for better relations with Cambodia. And we had blown it. The war was escalating with each passing day. The Communists increasingly used Cambodia not only as a route to infiltrate South Vietnam but as a sanctuary when the going got too hot on the other side of the border. The United States pleaded with Sihanouk to clean out these sanctuaries. But how could he? If the United States and the South Vietnamese army working together couldn't crush the VC on our side of the border, how could we expect the tiny Cambodian army to do it on their side?

Just three and a half years after I left Vietnam, on March 18, 1970, the pro-American Lon Nol overthrew Norodom Sihanouk while the prince was out of the country. Six weeks later, on April 30, the United States invaded Cambodia to wipe out the headquarters of the elusive Central Office of South Vietnam. We caused lots of damage but failed to find and crush the headquarters. Cambodia was now on the skids towards ruin. Five years later, the murderous Pol Pot would be running the country. I must admit that I never saw it coming. When the Khmer Rouge started killing everyone in sight, I could not believe it was happening in a country I once saw as a kind of Asian paradise.

*****

After my tour in Vietnam was over, Cambodia remained on my mind. Someday, I thought, I would visit the country I had only studied. But for a long time I didn't. At first I didn't have the money. Then, in 1975, the Khmer Rouge made it impossible. Unlike other 20th century mass murderers, the Khmer Rouge slaughtered their own people. I was not going near Cambodia while they were in power. In 1979, the Vietnamese communists finally kicked Pol Pot out of Phnom Penh. He and his merry band fled to the jungle where they continued to wage war for years after that.

My chance finally came in 1993. Mark Storella, a Foreign Service officer and close friend, was stationed in Phnom Penh. He invited me to spend a few weeks with him. The country I had fantasized about in 1966 was definitely not the country I saw in 1993. The lush scenery was still there, but little else was the same. Everywhere I turned, I saw armless or legless people begging in the streets. These poor souls generally worked the markets, the pagodas, and outside the hotels. These people had survived Pol Pot's regime only to lose a limb by stepping on a mine left over from the war. (There were untold numbers of these mines still buried under the ground. That explains why Cambodia has more amputees per capita than any other country in the world.)

The effects of the Khmer Rouge could be seen all over the country. In the beautiful seaside town of Kep, for example, the Khmer Rouge had destroyed all the villas including one once owned by Sihanouk. All that was left behind were blackened shells. Pol Pot's army didn't occupy the villas as most rational conquerors would have done. The Khmer Rouge just put them to the torch. I guess they couldn't achieve a 14th century agrarian paradise with these handsome villas still around.

Phnom Penh wasn't much better off. The capital's "Olympic" stadium was occupied largely by weeds and cats. A few athletes still jogged around the track, but the rest of the place looked like something out of a ghost town. The scoreboard over the huge swimming pool was burned out. The pool itself was half-filled with slimy rainwater. A few local kids thought it was OK for swimming. But the basketball arena and the tennis courts were all abandoned. As I stood at the top of the stadium and looked around, the scene looked like nothing so much as the end of the world. It was as if someone had dropped a neutron bomb on the place. All the people were dead, but the buildings remained.

VIETNAM FOLLIES
A Memoir of an Intelligence Officer

In 1966, this "Olympic" stadium had been the pride of Cambodia. The Southeast Asian games were once held there. The name showed that Sihanouk had visions of even grander events. In September of 1966, President Charles De Gaulle of France paid a visit to Sihanouk. The prince went all out to greet his distinguished visitor and, he hoped, benefactor. He ordered all secondary schools closed so the students could rehearse their greetings All the streets De Gaulle was likely to see were swept clean. The trees were painted white around the base to make them look more festive. Private homes along the motorcade route were all repainted. Flowerpots popped up out of nowhere. (Although I shared most of De Gaulle's views about the future of Southeast Asia and how to end the war, I didn't like him. To me he was a recovering colonist who should have kept his mouth shut.)

The grand finale of De Gaulle's visit was a visit to the Olympic Stadium. De Gaulle rode in an open limousine, with over 100,000 bright shining faces lining the streets to greet him. Like fans at a football game in the states, students flipped thousands of placards to produce a giant face of De Gaulle. The aging French hero did what he did best. He blasted the United States for the war in Vietnam. He embraced Sihanouk and the idea of a neutral Southeast Asia. The pair even issued a joint communique. De Gaulle didn't back up his words with deeds, however. All the prince got from this "great son of France" was a few new uniforms for his pitiful army, a new school, and a phosphate factory. Not exactly what Sihanouk had in mind.

Seeing the decayed and partly destroyed stadium was depressing enough. But my visit to Toul Sleng prison—the Auschwitz on the Mekong—made me wonder about membership in the human race. Toul Sleng hadn't always been a prison. It had once been the prestigious Toul Svay Prey High School. But in 1975, the Khmer Rouge turned the four-building school into Security Prison 21, or S-21. In one of the most unfathomable horrors of the 20th century, classrooms became prison cells and

Henry Billings

torture chambers. The genocide ended in 1979 when the Vietnamese invaders drove the Khmer Rouge back into the mountains. But the instruments of torture were still on display at Toul Steng. Faded bloodstains still mar the floors of the cells where prisoners had been chained to their beds and beaten with iron rods.

I tried closing my eyes and imaging kids laughing and running around in freshly-pressed school uniforms. It didn't work. One step inside the prison was all it took. The walls were covered with photographs of those who had been imprisoned here. My eye traveled to one of a typical Cambodian girl with innocent eyes and fragile body. Perhaps she was 14, perhaps only 11 or 12. She dressed in prison garb, her youth drained from her face. What had she done to deserve prison? Maybe her father was an army officer or her mother a schoolteacher. Or maybe she just wore glasses. In Pot Pol's mind, that was crime enough.

The Khmer Rouge had a simple goal. They wanted to rid their society of all decadence and corruption. They wanted to transform Cambodia into a utopian agrarian society. To them this meant purging anyone who symbolized modern culture. The educated—including women and children—were targeted. S-21 became one of the places where these people were rounded up and tortured. More than 17,000 victims passed through the prison. Like the Nazis before them, the Khmer Rouge kept careful records of their prisoners. They gave each one a number. They also took each person's picture on arrival. These are the photographs that cover the walls from top to bottom in several rooms. In one photograph, a mother holds her young child. Seemingly indifferent to the child in her arms, she looks impassively at the camera. Her expression was one of someone who had given up all hope.

One room contained paintings done by survivors of S-21. The art revealed in vivid colors the ordeals these people suffered. For example, they showed victims being stretched on a crude kind of rack. Others showed victims' heads being held under water. These, too, were hard to take. Another room featured a map of Cambodia covered with human skulls and bones with its rivers painted in blood red. (Some think this map, a work of Vietnamese propaganda, is in bad taste because it defiles the memory of the dead. They have urged the cremation of these bones with a traditional Buddhist ceremony. Others think the map serves as powerful evidence and a grim reminder of the crimes committed here.)

Toul Sleng's courtyard held nightmares of its own. Under the Khmer Rouge, the students' chinup bars were used to hang victims upside down with their heads in pots of water. This was done to torture rather than to kill. Signs posted around the courtyard warn inmates not to cry out while being tortured. I had to wonder what more the torturers could do. Suicide in such a place must have crossed every prisoner's mind. But the guards wouldn't allow it. They installed barbed wire over the 3rd floor windows to prevent inmates from jumping out.

The Khmer Rouge killed some people at S-21. But for the most part, they did their killing at a place called Choeung Ek, the infamous Killing Fields. During days of peak efficiency, the Khmer Rouge sent a 100 or so people a day to Choeung Ek, about 10 miles from downtown Phnom Penh. Here Khmer Rouge soldiers used farm hoes to smash in people's head. (This saved precious bullets.) The victims were then buried in what turned out to be 129 mass graves.

As with the French Revolution, this revolution eventually turned to consume its own. In the end, many of the victims of Toul Sleng and Choeung Ek were members of the Khmer Rouge. Some were even former guards who had inflicted torture on others. Part of me cheered this news. But mostly it just saddened me. The thing that struck me hardest was just how young the vast majority of victims and their torturers were. A great many on both sides of the thumb screws were easily young enough to have attended classes at Toul Svey Prey High School.

Henry Billings

Chapter 9 ~~ The Reds and the Blues

> Secretary of State Dean Rusk: *Senator [William Fulbright of Arkansas], is it not just possible that there is something wrong with them [the North Vietnamese]?*
>
> Senator William Fulbright: *Yes, there is something wrong with them… They are primitive, poor people who have been fighting for twenty years and I don't understand myself why they continue to fight, but they do."*
>
> A 1966 exchange in the Senate Foreign Committee

My third area of responsibility was enemy morale. Was it going up or down? Like "body counts" and roads interdicted and weapons captured, trying to evaluate enemy morale was part of our effort to quantify the war. Unlike those "objective" numbers, however, evaluating something as elusive as how someone we didn't even know was feeling about life and the war was a real pig in a poke.

No one could tell me exactly what "morale" meant. I figure there had to be thousands of little things that could make a person happy or sad. I knew that a rude remark, wet socks, no mail, and cold coffee were just a few of the ones that upset me. So what were we talking about? Deep down, I knew what the answer was supposed to be. Westmoreland had a vested interest in the concept of low enemy morale. In terms of showing progress, we needed to document that VC and NVA morale was going down. If we could prove that Charlie (the VC) and his northern comrades were feeling down in the mouth, it would indicate that we were winning the war. Declining enemy morale would lead to high VC desertion rates would lead to ultimate victory for the United States. For us, it was a golden opportunity

VIETNAM FOLLIES
A Memoir of an Intelligence Officer

for more self-deception. We were going to see only what we wanted to see.

On the surface, the case for declining morale wasn't hard to make—at least from our own preconceived notions. Every day I received a pile of captured enemy documents to read. For the most part they were Prisoner of War interrogation reports, interviews with VC and NVA defectors, personal journals and letters written home but never sent. In my view, the POW reports and the interviews were suspect. It wasn't that we couldn't learn anything from such documents, it was just that they presented a meaningless measure of morale. How many happy POWs would one expect to find? And I figured that defectors would say anything to their interviewers to win sympathy. So for me, the most revealing documents were the journals and letters found on captured or dead enemy soldiers. The writers of these documents had never expected their words to be read by strangers. The letters and journals were, therefore, the best measure of how these men honestly felt—at least at the time they were writing. Reading these documents also helped me to understand better the people on the other side of the war.

Before I got the documents, they were translated into English by various South Vietnamese translators. I had no way of knowing if meanings had been deliberately altered in any way to help prove a point or whether certain ideas had been "lost in the translation." Still, the journals and letters seemed genuine and I treated them as such.

Taking the evidence at face value, I reported that enemy morale was in the toilet and about to be flushed. (I've always wondered what the enemy would have said about *my* morale if they had read my letters.) The introduction of massive U. S. firepower and combat troops knocked the VC back on their heels. There was no doubt about that. Also, the Viet Cong worried that they might soon lose their support among the villagers. Our attacks in the air and on the ground had driven a wedge between the VC and the peasants. The villagers had to be saying to the VC, "What's this shit? We thought you could protect us."

The sudden display of massive American firepower might have even caused a flood of defections within the ranks of the VC. Many enemy soldiers became confused and frightened. One Viet Cong defector said in 1966, "It was a hard life. [At one time] there was not much bombing and strafing by the [South Vietnamese] Government. But after that, with the American helicopters and the American planes, we were constantly on the run. I had malaria. One day my mother sent friends to see me, begging me to return."

Many of the documents showed similar distress. It wasn't just the Viet Cong, either. The North Vietnamese troops had their own problems. They couldn't run home to Mama like the VC defectors could. At least, it wouldn't be easy. After all, they had already endured three months of slogging their way down the Ho Chi Minh trail. They had left their families hundreds of miles behind. Many of NVA soldiers were just teenagers. But others were family men with children. And, in the spirit of egalitarianism, there were female troops, too. Their letters back home told of the misery and loneliness they endured. Many became sick. Some died along the way. So, sure, their morale was sagging. Washington's men at Valley Forge had also had low morale. Still, they kept fighting. The Americans in the winter or 1777-1778 didn't give up and neither did the North Vietnamese and Viet Cong in the Vietnam War. But acknowledgment of their willingness to fight wasn't really the focus of my reporting. My job was to pull out direct quotes from the documents to prove an escalating "misery index."

While there were well-publicized desertions among both the VC and the NVA, there were never enough to destroy their will to resist. At the time I didn't understand how the VC and the NVA managed to stay so strong. In books written after the war, I learned that they just redoubled their indoctrination efforts. They held extra political training classes to make sure everyone kept

VIETNAM FOLLIES
A Memoir of an Intelligence Officer

his or her eye on the ball. As long as they believed in their "noble cause" and as long as they believed could outlast the Americans, the VC and the NVA leaders knew they would win in the end. In terms of pure psychological warfare, the communists outclassed us on every front. In Little League baseball there is something called the "mercy rule." The game is called off if one team is ahead by 10 or more runs after four innings. In Vietnam, we needed a mercy rule.

Freshly brainwashed, the VC and the NVA kept fighting despite overwhelming American firepower. The American military, on the other hand, spent a few hours at most explaining to our men why we were in Vietnam and why it was OK to die half a world away from home. It wasn't nearly enough. Americans have always been willing to risk their lives for their own "noble causes" but most of us didn't have a clue what this cause was in Vietnam. After the war, many veterans complained that they had never understood what they were fighting for.

That was never the case with the enemy. The North Vietnamese and the Viet Cong always knew exactly why they were fighting. Their leaders constantly reminded them. More than half their military training was devoted to political indoctrination. We might sneer at this "propaganda" but it worked. And the enemy wasn't just being fed a pack of commie lies. That would never have worked. The leaders appealed to people's sense of patriotism and nationalism. It was a plea that resonated with poorly-educated soldiers who knew nothing about imperialism or capitalism or Marxism. So communist leaders kept their message simple. "This is our country. We must throw out the foreign aggressors." On some basic level, most South Vietnamese would have accepted any kind of government *as long as it was Vietnamese.*

Huong Van Ba, a colonel in the North Vietnamese Army, was an ethnic southerner who went north in 1954 and reentered South Vietnam in 1964. He later said, *"*We had such hatred for the enemy and such devotion to the noble cause of liberating our suppressed people that we felt we could overcome any difficulty and make any sacrifice."

*****

The enemy never lost sight of the fact that the heart of Vietnam was in its villages. It was not in Saigon. At one time, 85% of the people lived in rural areas. Villages provided for all the basic needs of the people. Any villager always knew where to turn in times of trouble. In Saigon, there was no place to turn. Saigon was a city ruled by foreigners. In villages, however, there was a shared sense of trust, duty, and rights. Politics was local. Under the French, the government had ruled over villages with a gentle hand. The VC, too, understood the importance of villages. That was one reason why the rural population so overwhelmingly favored the VC.

This journal entry appeared in the May 9, 1966 issue of *Newsweek*. Written by Nguyen Quang Le, a North Vietnamese infiltrator, the entry was dated June 13, 1965. "Today we enjoyed only one meal because of the shortage of rice. We feel dog tired as we walk in the night. Over a stretch of 25 to 30 miles, the crimes of the U. S. imperialists are scattered here and there. The pine forest is charred by U.S. rockets. The bridges are blasted by U. S. bombs, the railroads melted and the houses burned. This fans the flames of hate in everyone."

Like many of the writers of these journals and letters, Le ended up dead. His last entry was on February 21, 1966. "The building of installations goes on in preparation for fighting." Soon after this, the journal fell into the hands of another enemy soldier who later defected to the South Vietnamese. Le's blood-stained journal was found among the possessions of this other soldier.

Reading such documents made me a bit uncomfortable. On the one hand, I had a job to do. I had to make an assessment of enemy morale. At the time I had no idea how effective the communists' political indoctrination classes really were. So it seemed to me that morale was bad and getting worse. The logical consequence of that was to push a little harder, bomb a little more, and then maybe they would quit or desert in droves.

On the other hand, reading this very personal stuff made me see the human face of the enemy. This was the part that kept me awake at night. In theory, I was supposed to hate these guys. They were the enemy. But many of the letters back home would have broken anyone's heart. I remember one soldier who was worried about his daughter's schooling. He gently scolded his wife, asking her to be sure the daughter was doing her homework. Other writers worried about the health of a grandparent or the damage done by a recent flood. Some of the captured documents were family photographs. They looked like something that might have been taken at any American photo studio—a smiling Mom and Dad with two well-scrubbed kids on their laps. Even though I was unmarried and had no children, it was hard for me not to put myself in their shoes. I found it increasingly impossible to demonize the Vietnamese in the same way we demonized the "Huns" in World War II or the "Japs" in World War I. But, of course, I tried to keep my own sentiments out of my reports. I had to be objective.

My reports documenting declining enemy morale were used by MACV as the basis for briefings given to visiting dignitaries. Over the course of the war, most journalists from Walter Cronkite on down and almost every member of Congress got a MACV briefing. My rank wasn't high enough for me to give these briefings myself, except to the lowest-ranking visitors. Colonel Gilliland took the spotlight for the VIPs. MACV artists made clever flip charts indicating falling morale. One visual aid has stuck in my head all these years. It was a caricature of a terrified VC with his head half out of a bunker as bullets zipped by his ear. These briefing were well rehearsed and very convincing. Most visitors walked away saying, "Wow, these guys really know what they're talking about." Not everyone, however, was dazzled. In 1968, Governor George Romney of Michigan, who was running for President, claimed that the army was trying to "brainwash" him with Saigon briefings. He never said he *was* brainwashed but that honest admission killed any presidential hopes he had.

*****

There was one aspect of enemy morale that would have long-term consequences. At the time, I missed its true significance completely. By 1966, large numbers of North Vietnamese troops had infiltrated into South Vietnam. These were not ethnic South Vietnamese coming back to their homes. I'm talking about ethnic North Vietnamese. Captured documents suggested friction between the VC and the NVA. Some VC thought that the NVA troops treated them condescendingly and got favored treatment from the leaders.

There was something to this. We all felt that the North Vietnamese and the South Vietnamese were wired differently. The Northerners seemed mostly to be stoic, hard-working drones. The Southerners were often corrupt but friendly party animals. We discovered just how deep the split between North and South really was only after the war ended. Northerners brushed aside Southerners even in Saigon. The Northerners ruled the South with an iron fist without even the pretense of a velvet glove. Former Viet Cong leaders were jailed or sent to reeducation camps or forced to flee the country.

Did we miss an opportunity to exploit this division? I don't think so. During the war the Viet Cong and the NVA were united against an external enemy far more than they were internally divided among themselves. Only after April 30, 1975, did the Northerners get their first real chance to degrade Southerners. Their belief in the coercive power of the state was too deep. It didn't allow for much in the way of basic freedoms or a live-and-

VIETNAM FOLLIES
A Memoir of an Intelligence Officer

let-live philosophy that once prevailed for the vast majority of people in Saigon.

*****

In the long run, the real issue wasn't enemy morale; it was our morale. It really didn't matter how low VC or NVA morale fell. Because the communists truly believed in their cause, they were willing to keep fighting indefinitely. That was not true of us. Only a handful of Americans were true believers in the domino theory. Only a few really believed that our "national security" actually rested on what happened in Vietnam. The rest of us were just along for the ride. That became more so as the war dragged on and the ranks were filled more and more by draftees fresh out of high school.

The old men in Washington who gave us this war did everything they could to keep up the morale of the young men. They wanted to make the war as painless as possible. That was why we had 12-month tours instead of longer ones. That was why we had the Bob Hope show. That was the reason why there was always plenty of ice cold beer, hot coffee, and cheap cigarettes nearby. It was why we got mail delivered every day. (And we got to write letters back home at no cost. All we had to do was write "Free" in the space where a stamp usually goes.) All the goodies at the PX were an attempt to provide as many stateside comforts as possible.

Although I never watched television during my year in Vietnam, it *was* available. One Air Force lieutenant colonel was quoted in *The New York Times* as saying, "When they told me last year (1965) in Washington to set up a television network in Vietnam, I thought it was, well, incongruous for a country at war."

Not incongruous enough. The United States announced a joint venture with South Vietnam to bring TV to the country by erecting a 25-kilowatt ground transmitter in Saigon with plans for a similar one in the Delta. TV became available on a limited basis. A transmitter was loaded onto a United States Navy Super Constellation plane called the Blue Eagle II. It circled Saigon every night to provide one hour of TV programming in Vietnamese and three hours in English. The military saw the new ground transmitter as a way to increase the availability of television and thus boost our morale. The army also saw the propaganda opportunities for the South Vietnamese government to convert more Vietnamese to their side. The flaw in this plan was evident. There were almost no TV sets in Vietnam. A handful of Americans had them, as did some of our SEATO allies. Beyond that, the only ones with TVs were top Vietnamese officials who were already joined at the hip with us. So although we starting importing more TV sets, the average Vietnamese never saw them. Francis Fitzgerald reported in 1966 that Vice President Hubert Humphrey donated a TV set and a generator for a project in Saigon's poor Eighth District. After the sun when down, that TV cast the only light around. No one else had electricity.

Televisions and cold beer notwithstanding, American morale would grow worse and worse as the war dragged on. We kept dying, but there was no real end in sight. Much of the blame for this was placed at the feet (often fleeing) of the South Vietnamese army. And indeed, the ARVN soldiers had the worst morale of all. Like the VC, they were supposed to be fighting for their country. But they rarely did. There were occasional exceptions, and these got plenty of play in the American media. Overall, however, these guys were the cut-and-run types. It didn't matter that they were equipped with all sorts of high-tech weaponry that far exceeded that of the enemy; they were not ready or willing to risk their own skin.

It wasn't hard to find the reasons. Other than a paycheck, most ARVN soldiers had little personal motivation to fight. The government offered them no better vision for the future. They had no higher principles fueling their hearts and minds. So they often deserted at will. In 1965, for example, over 113,000 South Vietnamese soldiers took a hike. By 1972, they were slipping away at a rate of 20,000 a month! Some apologists claimed that the South Vietnamese merely lacked "leadership." That was another of those damned half-truths of this war. Yes, they lacked leadership. The colonels and generals they had were mostly corrupt. (One popular form of corruption took the form of claiming to have more soldiers under their command than they actually did. Why would they claim nonexistent soldiers? They did it so they could pocket all those unclaimed paychecks. What this meant, however, was that they couldn't do the combat jobs they were assigned to do because they didn't have the manpower they claimed to have.) But it wasn't just leadership. The leaders in Saigon never built any bonds of trust with the peasants in the countryside. Their intelligence apparatus was inadequate. And the VC had so thoroughly penetrated their ranks that the enemy knew just about every move ARVN was about to make.

Despite these obvious deficiencies, official public criticism of ARVN was rare. No one in any administration wanted to admit openly that the South Vietnamese soldier was no match for the Viet Cong. Average American soldiers in the field knew the truth, however. They came to loathe our South Vietnamese allies. Americans noticed that their "Search and Destroy" operations were always risky and often deadly. Yet when the South Vietnamese army went on similar patrols, they almost never encountered the enemy. GIs scoffed at the South Vietnamese for their "Search and Evade" operations. The utter lack of fighting spirit among the South Vietnamese was a serious problem throughout the war. It was why we had to send combat units to Vietnam in the first place. And it was why Vietnamization was such a tragic failure at the end.

This inscription on a U.S. Army Zippo lighter sold in 1970 in Saigon sums it up best:

The Unwilling

Henry Billings

>   Working for the Unable
>   To Do the Unnecessary
>   For the Ungrateful

VIETNAM FOLLIES
A Memoir of an Intelligence Officer

Chapter 10 ~~ Down Time

"Sometime they'll give a war and nobody will come."
—Carl Sandberg, The People, Yes, 1936

All of us at the Research and Analysis Branch worked 84 hours a week. The other 84 hours were down time. A small part of that time was wasted sleeping—maybe 4 or 5 hours a night. Still, that left plenty of time to get into trouble in a city like Saigon. What an off-duty officer did depended on which shift he was working. If he worked the day shift, he was free to roam the streets of downtown Saigon after dark. That implied the kind of entertainment found mostly on Tu Do Street. Saigon's nightlife had a limited focus. It was centered on sex, and if you grew weary of that, there was always more sex. For every restaurant, there had to be at least a dozen massage parlors or "Saigon Tea" bars. The massage parlors were a fast in-and-out operation. The bars were different. Guys usually took girls back to their homes—in separate vehicles, of course. The women would stay for a few hours and then leave. They left before morning since it was safer that way. They knew there was no sense in advertising to their countrymen how they were making their living or with whom.

Things didn't always work out so smoothly, however. One evening my roommates and I had four young ladies over to the house for some light entertainment. But it seemed the police had followed the women to our house. Our guests hadn't been in the house more than a couple of minutes when we heard loud banging on the grated metal front door. Before we even got to the door, we saw gun barrels sticking through the small openings. It was the White Mice. They ordered the girls to leave right away. At first, we didn't know what to do. Nothing else

Henry Billings

like this had ever happened before. But the banging continued. There was no doubt in anyone's mind that these guys were serious. When we looked back at the women they had already begun to collect their belongings. They knew the score. They had to leave. Not wanting any trouble, they went peacefully. For sure, we didn't want any trouble either. And, in any event, there was nothing we could do to stop the police since they were armed to the teeth and had us outnumbered at least three to one. The way I figured it, a bunch of little guys with guns were going to beat four big guys with nothing.

We all thought it was an amusing story. No harm, no foul. (We had assumed that nothing bad happened to the girls and that they were simply released with a warning not to spent time in the homes of Americans.) But when we related the story to Colonel Gilliland the next morning, he blew a gasket. To him, the outrageous actions of the Vietnamese police were akin to an invasion of the United States Embassy. Our house was sacred ground—a piece of America. It represented home and apple pie. At first I thought he was kidding. But he wasn't. Gilliland actually wanted us to have taken on a dozen or so armed men with our bare hands. There was no way we were going to do that. Even if we had been armed – hell, even if we had had a rocket launcher aimed at the door – we would have acquiesced to the White Mice's demands. None of us wanted to kill or be killed in such a dispute.

"You should have resisted!" Gilliland shouted. "They had no right to enter the home of Americans!"

"But, sir, they had guns and we didn't"

"I don't give a shit. I don't want any cowards serving under me. The next time the fucking White Mice show up at your door, you better fight or else."

"Yes, sir."

We never found out what the "or else" meant because it never happened again. But if it had, no one would have been dumb enough to tell the colonel. None of us knew for sure what

VIETNAM FOLLIES
A Memoir of an Intelligence Officer

he would do. We did know that Colonel Gilliland was a bit of a loose cannon. He seemed to belong in the field killing commies more than he did behind a desk in Saigon. Rumor had it that once when he was in Hong Kong on R & R, he used the drain pipes outside his fifth-story hotel room to do chin-ups. I didn't doubt it. In the middle of MACV briefings, he was known to hop up on the table and bang out 20 push-ups, explaining to his stunned audience that he had to keep in shape. No, Gilliland wasn't anyone to mess with. For one thing, he held my life in his hands. If I pissed him off too much, he could have requested my transfer to a far more dangerous post. Even so, I came dangerously close on more than one occasion to going over the line.

*****

The night shift was safer. It was much easier to keep your nose clean when off-hours were daylight hours. We could play tennis or shoot hoops or play handball at the airport courts. Also, there were a few newly-built American swimming pools in town. There was a wonderful botanical garden and a zoo where we could get away from Saigon's smog-choked downtown streets. Sadly, as the war lingered on, the gardens and the zoo suffered from almost total neglect.

I was delighted to discover Saigon had a racetrack named Phu Tho just north of Cholon, the Chinese part of town. (I grew up in Somerville, Massachusetts, where every barroom and tobacco shop had its own bookie. My Dad played "the number" through his bookie faithfully every day for more than sixty years. As a product of my environment, I caught the gambling bug early. I often hopped on the MTA bus after high school to catch the last three afternoon horse races at Suffolk Downs. If I won, I might take the short subway ride to play the dogs at Wonderland that night. I figured it was part of my education as a street kid. In Vietnam, I missed racing so much I had my father send me the racing form from Suffolk and Wonderland so that I could keep track of my favorite horses and dogs.)

Phu Tho was something else again. It wasn't Santa Anita or even Suffolk Downs. In fact, it was hard to find if you didn't know exactly what you were looking for. Built in 1932, this small French Art Deco stadium was about half the size of a normal racetrack. Everything about Phu Tho was Lilliputian. The horses looked as if they belong in some country fair where toddlers could ride them for a dime around a thirty-foot circle. The horses – really just ponies—were no bigger than their plastic cousins on a Merry-Go-Round. Their size was the result of inferior breeding (mostly Mongolian ponies) and a poor diet. The jockeys were equally small, weighing at most 80 pounds. Most looked as if they were just 12 or 13 years old. I heard a rumor that many had to be tied to the saddle. Even then, some got tossed during the races. As at any track, it was never enough to have your horse finish first, it had to finish *with a jockey*.

The racing form was written in both French and Vietnamese. No handicapping help there. Instead I chose my favorites by watching the red dirt paddock. Did the jockey look like he could hang on for the entire race? Did the horse have both eyes open? Were there any obvious needle marks in the boy or the steed? The trick was to make a decision quickly. In the states, I would often wait until the last possible moment to bet because the odds were constantly changing. But at Pho Tho, only a certain number of tickets were sold on any given horse. So if you fancied number 5, you had to dash to the window to place your bet. If other people also liked number 5, there might be no tickets left. I discovered that the hard way. On my first day at Phu Tho, I liked number 3. When I went to the cage, there were no tickets left for that horse. "But we have plenty left on numbers 1, 4 and 5," said the teller. Of course, number 3 won in a romp while 1, 4 and 5 finished well up the track.

For me, the track was a harmless diversion. I imagined that all the races were fixed (a fairly safe assumption), but it was fun

VIETNAM FOLLIES
A Memoir of an Intelligence Officer

trying to guess the winner anyway and besides, I enjoyed watching the races and the people. The races themselves were mostly short—5 to 7 furlongs (these horses couldn't run much farther than that). And, as far as I could tell, there were no rules. The only safety precaution I noticed was the barbed wire around the track. The wire fence kept people far enough away from the rail so they couldn't throw stones at the horses they didn't want to win. Still, the horses often swerved left and right, banging into each at will. Horses fell all the time. No matter how rough the race was, no one ever claimed foul.

You certainly couldn't go broke at the window. The biggest single bet allowed was something like 10 or 20 piasters. On a bad day, you could lose four or five dollars on the races. A bigger threat was losing your wallet to one of the many pickpockets who worked the track.

Most of the people at the track were Chinese men. I swear they are the world's most compulsive gamblers. But there had to be some VC, too. I knew that horse racing wasn't part of the communist game plan. But the track itself was, although I didn't know it at the time. I was surprised to learn that during the Tet Offensive, communists used Phu Tho as a command post and a field hospital. (After the war, the track was deserted for many years. There was no gambling allowed under Hanoi's rule. But in the 1990's, the government eased up and allowed the track to reopen for a couple of days a week. It's still a small rat trap, but on Sundays as many as 30,000 people show up to bet on the ponies.)

*****

While I enjoyed the ponies, my favorite "down time" haunt was the Saigon Country Club. For one thing, the clubhouse cafe served the best noodle soup in town. For another, in case of a MACV emergency, I would be hard to find. And, besides, golf is golf. Of course, I wasn't sent to Vietnam to play golf. Before I

Henry Billings

knew I had landed a soft desk job, I'd thought I would be sleeping under the stars and burning leeches off my forearm with a cigarette. Instead, though, I found myself burning up the fairways like Colonel Henry Blake of M*A*S*H. (The VC apparently liked the course, too. They used a textile mill just behind the seventh green as their main command post during the Tet Offensive.)

The Saigon Country Club was a nine-hole course that had been transformed into an 18-hole course. The extremely narrow fairways were stacked side by side like a collection of swizzle sticks. You were able to stand on the eighth green and see the other 17 flags. I wasn't much of a golfer, so most of the time I ended up hitting off the wrong fairway. My real problems came on holes along the outside edge of the course, where there were houses to the right. With my natural slice, I bounced quite a few balls off the corrugated metal roofs.

The Saigon Country Club was actually two courses in one—the dry-season course and the wet-season course. The dry course was five or six stokes harder to play. So we needed a separate handicapping system for each, much as you might handicap mudders in horse racing. When the weather was dry, it was really dry: the course was flat and it played like the top of a pool table. A low, hard drive would strike the fairway and take off as though it had landed on an interstate highway. On the greens (called browns during the dry season), a missed three-foot putt on the slightest downhill grade meant a return putt of 10 feet. The greens were mostly flat and hard as diamonds, and sometimes it was impossible to tell where the fairway ended and the green began. From about 50 yards on in, you could use your putter.

In the wet season, on the other hand, every shot was a water shot. It was wise to bring along an extra pair of socks. Fairway rolls were unheard of, and the greens held like a swamp. In that dense, humid atmosphere, even well-stroked shots fizzled and died like a child's emptying balloon. A five-iron shot in the dry season might be a two-iron shot in the wet season.

Tee times were never a problem. Often my golfing buddies and I would have the whole course to ourselves. The Vietnamese didn't play golf, and I don't think the enlisted men gave the game much thought. In truth, you really had to like the game because the course was in rough shape. I don't think I ever saw a maintenance worker. The bunkers were hard enough to bend the shaft of a sand wedge. Drainage trenches crisscrossed the fairways. Tee areas were selected by general consensus among the golfers, not by management.

A lost ball didn't remain lost for long. A small army of Vietnamese kids would collect the balls and resell them to the players. I can still see those tiny unwashed hands sticking through the wire fences, offering five or six balls—including, often, one of my own. We didn't object to this, since it was honest labor and there was no other way to retrieve a ball hit over the fence. Also, decent golf balls were scarce. Most of us had them shipped from the States.

Sometimes, however, the local kids didn't play by the rules. They didn't wait for an out-of-bounds shot. The kids took the matter of supply and demand into their own hands. They would hide in the bushes about 200 yards down range and pounce on the ball when it landed. Once, on a par-5, I hit a terrific 3-wood that came down in front of the green and rolled to within three feet of the pin. Eagle City. Before I could shout my joy, a barefooted urchin dashed onto the green and made off with my ball. My playing companion, standing less than 10 feet from me, claimed that he never saw the shot and that the only fair thing to do would be for me to hit again—and he generously offered not to assess a penalty for the lost ball. What a prince. I ended up with an 8 on the hole. To add insult to injury, the next day the little thief tried to sell that eagle putt ball back to me. All I could do was laugh and pay him his money.

Henry Billings

Like Phu Tho, the Saigon Country Club was surrounded by barbed wire with small holes poked through by the "ball" boys. Whoever had the concession on barbed wire must have made a fortune. But after a few swings, no one noticed notice the wire much unless the ball landed next to it and it interfered with the next swing.

We tended to zone out on the sound of thumping choppers and roaring jet fighters as well as the occasional explosion. We stopped worrying about terrorism. Most of us shared a common sense of fatalism in that regard. If the Viet Cong wanted to get us, all they had to do was rig the ball washer with plastique. Or they just could lob a few mortar rounds in our direction or fire at us from the roof of a neighboring home. We were never quite sure we would finish our round but we didn't worry about it. Of course, the Saigon Country Club wasn't the Central Highlands or Khe Sanh or the Iron Triangle, but it was at least as dangerous as Central Park in New York City.

Near the end of my tour, I played golf often. My replacement had been trained and I had the last few days off. Then, on November 1, 1966, I almost joined the real war. It was a little after 7 o'clock in the morning. I was addressing the ball on the first tee. Just as I reached the top of my backswing, I heard a huge explosion. Then another and another. The VC had launched a recoilless rifle attack on Saigon. This was the first time during the war that they had shelled downtown Saigon. One shell hit the steeple of the Basilica of Our Lady, the largest Catholic church in town, killing a priest instantly and spraying glass and mortar onto the street below. At the same time, a terrorist lobbed a grenade into a crowded bus terminal near the Central Market. Also, the VC mined and sank a U. S. Navy minesweeper on the Langtau River, Saigon's main link to the sea. The surprise attack caused widespread panic on the streets of Saigon, with people everywhere scurrying for cover.

The Viet Cong timed the attack to coincide with South Vietnam's National Day parade honoring the fallen Ngo Dinh

VIETNAM FOLLIES
A Memoir of an Intelligence Officer

Diem. All the major players on our side took part in the celebration. Prime Minister Nguyen Cao Ky was there. So, too, was General Westmoreland and a large group of visiting dignitaries.

They should have been sitting ducks. But the Viet Cong apparently forgot to reset their watches. They had forgotten that Hanoi time is one hour different than Saigon time. (For such terrific fighters in general, the VC sometimes acted a few pennies short of a dime.) So the attack came before everyone had gathered in the reviewing stands. To make up for the mistake, the VC fired a few more shells an hour later, but did little damage.

"Nobody move even if we get killed!" shouted Ky when he heard the first explosions from the second attack.

The first attack had killed about 20 people, including one American. As things went in this war, it was not a big deal. But it was certainly a warning shot across the bow. The VC pulled off this shelling without losing a single man. Their actions demonstrated just how vulnerable Saigon was to attack. But we and our South Vietnamese allies weren't willing to admit it. The spin we put on the whole episode was that the attack was a sure sign we were winning the war. Wasn't everything? The shelling proved just how desperate the enemy was and that they would do anything to boost their morale.

Back at the Saigon Country Club, I continued to play my round. There was nothing I could do, anyway. The attack brought out so many army helicopters from Tan Son Nhut that they just about blotted out the sun. I could look up and see machine gunners loading their weapons right by the open door. One soldier reached down and almost grabbed my second shot on the first hole, a 9-iron headed right for the pin.

Henry Billings

Chapter 11 ~~ The Loving Cup

"The only thing that ever consoles man for the stupid things he does is the praise he always [gets] for doing them."
—Oscar Wilde (slightly modified), 1890

Esprit de corps wasn't something that flowed naturally out of the gang at the Research & Analysis Branch. After all, none of us walked point on a night patrol through the bush or watched a friend bleed to death because a rescue helicopter was late. We were basically office workers—rear echelon people more likely to suffer from carpal tunnel syndrome than combat fatigue. How much spirit of brotherhood can be squeezed out of that? Not much. Of course, Colonel Gilliland had other ideas. He saw us as his intellectual fighting force. So as a bonding experience, each month Gilliland had us vote and award one officer something called *The Loving Cup*. This ritual, along with a monthly office party at the Continental Hotel, was supposed to bring us all a little closer together. I guess the hope was that with the right trappings, we'd seem more like the soldiers who were doing the actual fighting.

The Loving Cup had nothing to do with sex. No, it was a satirical prize given to the one who "loved" Vietnam the most. In other words, the cup went to the officer who had just had the most miserable month. It could be because of something personal or professional or a mix of the two. I thought I would win hands down every month and that they would be forced to retire the cup with my name on it. But other guys hit rough patches too. The first month, I lost out to the officer who had written that first overly-optimistic B-52 report and had been roundly criticized for it. I lost the next month to a Mormon. I don't recall his particular misfortune, but I do remember that he was as out of place in Vietnam as I was.

I didn't set out to win *The Loving Cup*. I had no grand strategy in mind. Still, I knew that if I just did things the way I usually did them, I would win sooner or later. Well, it came sooner and the vote was unanimous. My credentials began building one steamy Saigon night. I decided to take a short walk to a bridge near our house. My initial impulse was just to visit the bridge, take in the view, and go back to the house to sleep. I didn't think about how I was dressed. It turned out I had on a plain white T-shirt and a pair of army pants. While on my walk, I changed my mind and decided to grab a cyclo to Cholon for a little bar hopping in the Chinese section of town. It was no big deal. I was just killing time.

While in one bar, I met some other officers from MACV. I remember one of them saying, "Nice uniform." I had no idea what in the world he was talking about, so I basically ignored him. After a few hours and a half dozen beers, I decided to go home. I left the bar and walked down the street looking for an available cyclo. Just as I hailed one, two American MPs stopped me.

"Soldier," one of them said, "Look at yourself."

I looked down and saw nothing wrong. My fly was buttoned. My shoes were tied. What was their point?

"You're out of uniform!" one of them barked at me.

"Huh?" I must have looked as dumb as a bag of hammers because I still had no idea what they were talking about.

Never strong on military etiquette, it took me several seconds to realize what "out of uniform" even meant. I didn't often think in those terms. But slowly the light dawned. If I had been wearing civilian pants instead of army ones, it wouldn't have been a problem. On the other hand, if I had worn my army shirt and tie and hat, that too would have been fine. But I was in army pants and a civilian shirt. So I really wasn't "out of uniform." The truth was I was "half in and half out of uniform."

Henry Billings

"Ah, yes, I see what you mean," I stuttered at last.

"Soldier, you're under arrest."

With that, they shoved me in the back of their jeep and headed for the military police barracks. I knew the shit was really going to hit the fan when Gilliland found out. He was a real stickler for proper dress. As we zipped through the streets of Cholon, one of the MPs asked me for my identification card. I reached into my wallet and handed it over.

"He's an officer!" the MP called to the one who was driving. They were flabbergasted that an officer didn't know how to dress properly. Suddenly, their whole attitude changed. I was still under arrest, but they were much more respectful now. All along they had assumed I was a dumb enlisted man. After all, without an army shirt, they had no way of knowing that I was a dumb officer. And they had probably never seen an officer, even a lowly lieutenant, out of uniform.

Still, they had me dead to rights. Officer or no officer, they had a clean arrest. Nothing much would have happened to me, of course, as far as the Military Police were concerned. Maybe a small fine or a black mark on my efficiency report. But Gilliland was something else. If he had found out that night and decided to take matters into his own hands, I still shudder to think what he might have dreamed up.

But I got lucky. For some reason, the MPs took pity on me. (On the jeep ride I tried to explain what happened. It was just an innocent mistake.) Instead of taking me to the MP barracks, they took me back to my house and suggested I change my pants or put on the complete uniform. Nice guys, those MPs. I thanked them and went to bed.

Word of my misadventure quickly spread through the office from those in the bar who saw me being arrested in Cholon. But Gilliland didn't get wind of it until much later. The "arrest" by itself would have insured my winning *The Loving Cup*. But I was about to became a minor legend at Tan Son Nhut airport.

VIETNAM FOLLIES
A Memoir of an Intelligence Officer

*****

My work on enemy morale continued, with more interrogation reports of captured enemy soldiers to read every day. Up until now, all the reports had been sent directly to me. But one day Colonel Gilliland told me to go to one of the prisons in Saigon myself. I don't recall the details of the mission but I do remember that I was to bring some highly classified materials with me. It was the first time he had ever asked me to do something like that. There wouldn't be a second time.

Anyone carrying Top Secret papers must exercise a high degree of care in transporting them. Security was vital. So I was supposed to carry a sidearm and keep the papers locked in a briefcase. I might have locked the briefcase to my wrist or to some part of the jeep.

Naturally, I took a rather cavalier attitude toward such regulations. I carried no gun. I used no fancy briefcase. And I brought along no locks. Instead I put the papers in a plain manila folder on the seat next to me as I took off in Gilliland's jeep. The R & A Branch had two jeeps at the airport—Gilliland had one and Major Stromgrin, his assistant and second in command, had the other. The rest of us borrowed them according to rank and need. Since I was one of the lowest-ranking officers, I had never driven Major Stromgrin's jeep. And certainly this was the first time Gilliland had let me behind the wheel of his vehicle.

As I drove through the streets of Tan Son Nhut, the sudden wind caught the top of the manila folder and the Top Secret documents began blowing around on the seat. I said to myself, "Oh, shit! Don't do that!" I quickly glanced over and smashed my hand down on the top of the flipping folder. Too late. Some of them had already flown out of the jeep. As I leaned over to my right to close the folder, I naturally pulled the steering wheel in the same direction. Big mistake. When my eyes turned back to the road, all I saw was a huge sign. It read: *Drive Carefully! Per Order of the Base Commander*.

Henry Billings

Wham! I smashed right through that sign. Knocked it clean off its moorings. And that wasn't the half of it. Just past the sign was a low concrete block with a thick cable attached to it. I was going fast enough to crash through the sign and hit that concrete block – and even to snap the cable. The jeep might have emerged on the other side of the sign with only few scratches, but it didn't stand a chance against the concrete block. The crash bent the frame and—in effect—totaled the jeep. Before long, a crowd had gathered to see if I was all right and to inspect the damage.

Amazingly enough, I wasn't badly injured. I had banged up my knee a bit but was otherwise OK. My initial concern wasn't for my knee or the jeep; it was for all those secret documents that were now floating with the breeze here and there. An accident is one thing. That could happen to anyone. But losing Top Secret documents was a whole new ball game. I couldn't begin imagine the number of security violations that might be lodged against me by the army. And I didn't want to find out. So I began dashing around like a madman, trying to get all of the papers back in the folder.

At last I collected all the sensitive documents. For a few minutes, that seemed to be the end of the story. I'd had a simple stupid accident made mildly humorous by the message on the demolished sign. But there was one more shoe still to fall. Someone began pointing down a short dead-end side street running perpendicular to the main road. The concrete telephone poles along this narrow street had suddenly toppled over. One hit the hood of a pickup truck, another hit a Vietnamese food cart, another hit a bicycle, and the last one narrowly missed the tail of a parked plane.

None of the people buzzing around me could figure out why the poles had fallen over. There seemed to be no apparent connection between the accident and the toppled poles. After all, the first fallen pole had to be at least 100 feet away. But as I looked down that street, I felt a sickening wave wash over me. I knew why those poles had toppled. The wire cable that my jeep had snapped had been holding all those poles up. I don't know whether the French strung the telephone wires that way or whether it was the Vietnamese, but the poles were not individually set into the ground the way telephone poles in my old neighborhood were. So when I broke the cable, all the poles fell over. It was a miracle that none of them had killed anyone.

If ever anyone needed a State Farm agent, it was me. I was facing a financial disaster. The jeep alone was worth more than my pay for the entire year in Vietnam. I had no idea how much the dead-end street damage might cost, but it looked significant. Given the fact that I didn't want to be in Vietnam in the first place, my immediate impulse was to flee the scene and never look back. I had a week's R & R trip to Kuala Lumpur coming up soon; I could just go to Malaysia and never return—like a different Charlie on the MTA. I was perfectly willing to become an expatriate and spend the rest of my life in Asia. Still, before I could pursue this escape fantasy, I knew I would have to deal with the fact that I had just wrecked Colonel Gilliland's jeep. I didn't think he would be amused.

The colonel was sitting at his desk when I approached. "Sir," I said straightforwardly. "I just wrecked your jeep." He never looked up. He just put down his pen and stuck out his hand.

"Let me see your license," he said.

I reached into my wallet and pulled out my military license. Without a word, the colonel took the license, ripped it neatly in half, and handed the two pieces back to me. "Your driving days are over," he said softly.

I had half expected him to haul off and deck me on the spot. But this was a gentler, kinder Gilliland. He was milking the situation. The office by now was crowded with every member of the R & A Branch.

Gilliland turned to Major Stromgrin, who was sitting nearby at his desk. "Major," he said, "Let me have the keys to your jeep."

With a look of surprise, Stromgrin handed over his keys.

Henry Billings

Gilliland looked back at me and said, "Lieutenant, you didn't wreck my jeep, you wrecked Major Stromgrin's jeep."

If only the army could have bottled the look Stromgrin gave me, we would have had a new weapon to use on the enemy.

*****

The U.S. Army ordered a Report of Survey on the jeep. The initial word was that I would have to pay for the whole jeep. I was told that the price for a new jeep was $7,777. My total pay for a year in Vietnam was less than $6,000. But luckily, someone took mercy on me. Although the jeep was totaled, the army charged me only what it would have cost to fix the jeep—if it had been fixable. In other words, I had to pay for the bent frame. That turned out to be only a few hundred dollars. To collect the money, the army garnished my pay. (Strangely, I never heard a word about the damage caused on the side street. I didn't hide but then again I didn't go looking for victims, either.) I would not have to run away to Malaysia after all. By a very thin margin I remained a patriot—a humbled and embarrassed patriot but a patriot all the same. For the next several weeks, I often overheard conversations in the officers' club about the asshole who drove through the *Drive Carefully: Per Order of the Base Commander* sign.

Naturally, that month I won *The Loving Cup* by acclamation. The R & A guys didn't bother going through the formality of a vote. The award was given to me at a party held in a back room at the Continent Hotel. The booze flowed freely. Now soberly embedded in my middle age, I can only look back in wonder at how much I was then able to drink and still remain standing. Liquor boosts one's courage and also loosens one's tongue. I chose my acceptance speech as the occasion to relate to Colonel Gilliland my other qualification of *The Loving Cup*—the arrest in Cholon. Photos taken immediately after my speech showed that the colonel was not a happy camper. But he decided to let it slide. What else could he do with a sad sack like me?

Henry Billings

Chapter 12 ~~ Taking Leave

"Wrong and morally wrong in its conduct and consequences, [the Vietnam War] was nevertheless not evil in intent or origin.
What propelled us into this war was a corruption of the generous, idealistic, liberal impulse."
—Alexander M. Bickel in The Morality of Consent, 1975

I may have scoffed at Colonel Gilliland's rituals, but I had one of my own. As each day ended, I crossed out the date on my pocket calendar. There was no number I knew better than the number of days I had left in Vietnam. Despite the fact that I actually liked Vietnam and had a low-risk job, I didn't want to be part of the war. If I had sensed that the war was wrong before I left the States, the things I saw and learned during my tour only solidified my views. I wanted out. My year couldn't end fast enough. Sometimes I would draw a single line through the date at noontime—half a day gone. Late at night I would complete the X. In my spare time, I did all the possible mathematical calculations—percentage of time served versus percentage of time left, number of days left, number of hours, and so forth.

At the Research & Analysis Branch we celebrated certain landmarks. At the halfway point of our tour, we had an "over-the-hump party." We had "short-timer" parties for those near the end of their tour. If a guy had less than a month to serve, he was short. If he had less than a week to go, he was really short. All these landmarks were reasons to party. We grasped at any excuse to kick back, have a few drinks and forget the war.

Since many of us arrived on the same date, our tours ended at the same time. We didn't all leave on exactly the same day. That would have been too disruptive. Instead, we left in twos and threes over a period of a couple of weeks. In any case, in early November, 1966, we scheduled a real blow-out party. During our year "in country," we had added to our staff, but more than half of us were going home in November. Colonel Gilliland decided to honor the event by suggesting that everyone who was leaving be given a plaque commemorating his service to the war effort in Vietnam. To pay for the plaques, he asked for a voluntary office collection.

This was my last, and most bitter, conflict with the colonel. I flatly refused to contribute a dime to pay for the plaques. I also refused to accept the one intended for me. I didn't tell the colonel this directly, of course. But when the collection plate came around, I said, "No, thanks." I told the collecting officer that he needn't raise as much money as he'd been told, since I didn't want a plaque. To me, the plaque seemed to glorify war and I wanted no part of it. My views had really hardened over my year in Vietnam. I had lost all sense of "going along to get along."

Looking back now, I realize that Colonel Gilliland meant no harm. It was his way of honoring all the officers under his command for their service to the United States. But I just couldn't see it that way at the time. I wanted no honors—however slight and well-intended—for taking part in this war.

My stance won me no support whatsoever among the others in my office. So it wasn't surprising that word of my non-participation filtered back to Gilliland. He saw my refusal as a direct challenge to his authority and to army life in general. He promptly called an emergency meeting of all the officers. I had no idea what he was up to. The colonel never tipped his hand early. But it soon became clear. Once we were all gathered together, he launched into a sermon—it really was a sermon—about *esprit de corps*. Gilliland gave us a brief history lesson about his own past service and how his different units had pulled together. He talked about the importance of team unity and how a chain is only as strong as its weakest link and so on. Then,

Henry Billings

without ever mentioning my name and the plaque issue, he said that he would not tolerate anyone in his unit who lacked *esprit de corps*. These words were barely out of his mouth when I stood up and said, "Colonel, I will not contribute to any plaque fund and I will not accept any plaque!"

You could heard a pin drop. The colonel slowly turned his gaze on me and said through clenched teeth, "Report to my office immediately." The meeting was over.

Everyone filed out, whispering softly to each other.

I had less than a week left in my tour, so why did I openly challenge the man? I don't know. Sometimes I just blurted things out without thinking. But as I walked into Gilliland's office, I knew this was no defense.

Gilliland was purple. He dressed me up and down about respect and obedience and the war effort. With all the new guys coming in, he didn't want me setting a bad example. This war wasn't a picnic, he said. America's commitment was growing daily. But the whole effort could be undermined by poor morale and the lack of *esprit de corps*.

As Gilliland ranted, all I wanted to do was disappear. Just sink into the floor and vanish. Since that wasn't possible, I stood at attention and weathered the storm. In the end, the colonel knew he couldn't force me to pay for the plaques. He did, however, have the power to order me to accept a plaque with my name on it. "That's a *direct order*," he said. I saluted, turned and left the office.

I accepted the plaque at a huge bash in downtown Saigon. I was a nervous wreck all day. I honestly didn't know, when push came to shove, whether I would accept the plaque. I finally decided to do so, but in my own way.

That afternoon, I drank steadily to calm my nerves. I was totally in the tank by the time the presentations were made. As the other guys got their plaques, they all made little speeches highlighting their gratitude, humility, and patriotism. Finally it was my turn. I don't recall the exact words I spoke but it was

VIETNAM FOLLIES
A Memoir of an Intelligence Officer

something to the effect that I would accept the plaque only as a token of friendship. I would not consider it a reward for participating in a war I didn't believe in. With everyone else watered to the gills, no one seemed to notice or care. My act was getting old and, besides, I would be leaving in a few days. Even Colonel Gilliland said nothing. When I got home later that night, I looked at the plaque for the first time. The Vietnamese craftsman who had made it had left out the second r in the word "Research." Turns out it wasn't just my plaque that had the error; they all did. I took that as a small victory.

Two days later, I boarded the "freedom bird" for home. It was a Pam Am 707 loaded with a couple of hundred soldiers. They all cheered as the wheels lifted off the runway. I didn't. I kept thinking about how easy it would be for the Viet Cong to shoot down the plane. I waited until we banked out over the South China Sea and then I quietly pumped my fist in the air.

*****

Several of my friends were on the same flight, but when we reached the West Coast we all went off in separate directions. So when my plane touched down in New Jersey, I was alone. Although I was in uniform, I was just another passenger in the terminal. There were no bands, no parades, no flags, no nothing. That, of course, was fine by me. And just for the record, no one spat on me, either.

From New Jersey I grabbed a regular commercial flight for Boston. I switched into civilian clothes for the flight. All my Massachusetts relatives were at Logan Airport to greet me. My three-year old nephew, John Henry, ran up to me and asked, "Uncle Henry, where's your uniform and medals?"

In his eyes I was some kind of conquering hero. Not wanting to disappoint him, I said, "The army won't let me fly in uniform because I'm a secret spy. Don't tell anyone."

"O. K. Uncle Henry."

Henry Billings

Everyone else was just happy I had returned in one piece. They were proud, too. (None of them knew how I really felt about the war.) I found out just how proud they were a couple of days later when I took my Mom and Dad to Suffolk Downs for dinner and an evening of harness racing. I wore a sports coat with an open-collar shirt. We walked into the clubhouse restaurant and took an empty table. Within a minute or so, the maitre d' approached us and said that I would have to leave because I wasn't wearing a tie. (Dad was. He always wore a tie.)

Before I could say a word, Dad exploded. He almost never got mad. Troubles always seemed to roll off him like water off a duck's back. Not this time, however. He screamed something about how I had just returned from Vietnam and had fought to save the country from communism and how dare this poor excuse of a human being kick me out of this flea bag restaurant simply because I wasn't wearing a tie. It was one of Dad's finest moments. Suddenly, out of nowhere, a tie appeared. We enjoyed the rest of the evening and actually won some bucks when a 20 to 1 shot named Lieutenant Gray won.

*****

Flying home in small groups or even one at a time pointed out how different Vietnam was from other U. S. wars. In Vietnam, most soldiers trained separately from those with whom they would serve. They went to war as individuals and returned—if they did—as individuals. So there was little in the way of unit cohesion. By way of contrast, during the Civil War, boys from their hometowns or their home states formed their own units. They trained together, fought together, and came home together. In World War I and World War II, although the units were not based on hometowns or states, men still trained together, fought together, and came home together when the war was over.

VIETNAM FOLLIES
A Memoir of an Intelligence Officer

I was lucky in this regard. Because I went to Vietnam early in the conflict, I got to go with my unit. I trained with the men I served with. Our replacements always came as individuals. Because of the short 12-month tour, every unit—combat as well as support—had old guys leaving and FNGs (fucking new guys) arriving all the time. Obviously, it was no way to fight a war. As soon as a man got his feet wet and really understood his job, he was sent back home and replaced by a novice who had to start the learning process all over again. In this regard I have to tip my hat to Colonel Gilliland. He tried to build a feeling of all-for-one-and-for-all and he openly regretted losing so many experienced intelligence analysts within a week or so.

But my job in November 1966 wasn't to tell the army how to run their war. My interest was to finish my two-year stint in the army and go back to civilian life. I was stationed back at Fort Devens in Massachusetts where I had taken my summer ROTC course. Upon arrival, I became second in command of a Replacement Company which helped to reassign people to new units. It was a soft job. Basically, I had to sign a few papers and break in the new pool table for the recreation hall.

I left the U. S. Army in August of 1967. By that time I really missed Vietnam – the country. As much as I hated the war, that year was the most exciting of my life. Life in the United States seemed dull and colorless in comparison. So I decided to go back. Not as an army officer, however. I still opposed the war with all my heart. I decided to go back as a civilian aid worker in some rural village in South Vietnam. I applied for a job with an agency—I've forgotten which one—and they turned me down. I was rejected out of hand because I had been an intelligence officer. Next I applied to the Peace Corps. I figured if I couldn't go back to Vietnam, maybe I could go to Africa or South America. Like many twenty-somethings of that era, I had a powerful desire to "do good" but in an exotic locale. Again, no dice. The Peace Corps wouldn't even let me explain that I wasn't really a spy. The mere implication of "intelligence" work was enough to kill my application.

At first, I tried to just forget the war. It wasn't my problem anymore. But there was no escaping it. It was on page one every day. It led the TV evening news broadcasts most nights. After a while I began going to anti-war rallies. I wanted to lend a hand in the movement to end the war. In October 1967, I attended a draft-card burning service at the Arlington Street Church in Boston. A group of young protesters met on the Commons and marched to the church. Along the way, people waving American flags and pro-war signs shouted and spit at us and called us cowards and traitors. (There was still general support for the war even as late as the fall of 1967. Ironically, people spat at me *not* for being a baby-killer or a village-burner but for not having the guts to serve in the military.) The march and draft-card burning, organized by liberal church leaders, was nonviolent and I don't recall anyone getting arrested that day.

Later, I went to more violent protests organized by returning combat veterans who had turned against the war. Many of these veterans had obvious injuries. Some were in wheelchairs. And all were bitter about their experience. They wore parts of their uniforms as well as love beads and long hair. I shared their anger about the war. I even went so far as to send the five medals I had earned to the White House with a note telling President Nixon what he could do with them.

But with those combat veterans, I remained on the fringe of the crowd. Their war was not my war. These men had seen and done things that I could never imagine. So after a while, I stayed away. I was a Vietnam veteran but there was this void. I was but I wasn't. Still, the experiences I had brought an insider's view to how we were fighting the war. As a high school teacher and later as a freelance writer, I told just bits and pieces of my story until now.

*****

VIETNAM FOLLIES
A Memoir of an Intelligence Officer

I did keep in touch with many of the men I served with in Vietnam. We even held a five-year reunion in Washington D. C. But, slowly, over the years, these contacts broke off and we drifted apart. Now I am in touch with just one member of the old Research & Analysis Branch. Captain Joe Arden, our resident Ph.D. in Saigon, stayed in Asia after his tour was over to work as a teacher for the Asian branch of the University of Maryland. He taught army personnel college courses in history and political science, bouncing around from one Asian capital city to another. Joe would teach 10 weeks in Tokyo, then 10 weeks in Bangkok, followed by 10 weeks in Taipei or Manila and so on. It was an addictive way of life and he loved it. For a long time I envied him and his freedom. Joe eventually became the administrative head of the University of Maryland in Asia.

Still, although we shared a war together, I don't think we bonded together the way, say, the members of the 101st Airborne did after World War II. For one thing, being a Vietnam veteran wasn't a popular thing to be for many years. World War II was the good war; Vietnam was the bad war. So we didn't advertise our past. No one I know, for example, joined the VFW. (We all got the applications to join while we were still in Vietnam. I just laughed and tossed mine into a wastebasket, never giving it another thought.) Also, we weren't in combat. None of us saved anyone else's life. In addition, we only served a year together. That said, I still wonder what happened to many of my old friends and what they think about the Vietnam War now that so many years have passed.

Henry Billings

Chapter 13 ~~ Going Back

"Vietnam is a country, not a war"
—new slogan to encourage American tourism

I had left Vietnam but Vietnam never left me. That doesn't mean I suffered from any post-war stress syndrome. I wasn't depressed about my experiences. I didn't need any psychological counseling to reenter civilian life. And I didn't wear my old army shirt every day as some anti-war veterans did. While I did—like most people from that time—experiment a bit with marijuana, drugs were not an issue and soon left my life for good. So I wasn't a war-shattered vet. There was no reason to be. I had waltzed my way through Vietnam. The only time I felt emotional pain was when I visited the Vietnam Memorial Wall and ran my fingers along the name of George Birdsell. That really shook me.

Thoughts about Vietnam, the country, were never far away, however. I wanted to go back to see the place again when it wasn't a war zone. But money and circumstances kept me from doing that for a long, long time. Then, in 1993, I saw my chance. While visiting my Foreign Service friend Mark Storella in Cambodia, we decided to fly to Saigon for a couple of days. Getting into Vietnam at that time wasn't easy. Relations between the United States and Vietnam were still badly strained. We had to jump through a number of hoops to get the right papers and permits.

Confident that we were all set, we boarded an Air Kampuchea plane for the short hop from Phnom Penh to Saigon. You really have to be anxious to go someplace if you're willing to fly on Air Kampuchea. We're talking about the bottom of the food chain here. The plane we flew was a *used* Russian plane. (Apparently, the Russians unloaded their oldest and least sky-worthy planes on Cambodia.) I tried not to speculate on who, if anyone, was in charge of its maintenance. After all, hadn't the Khmer Rouge killed anyone who could read a maintenance manual?

I'm not a fearful flyer. But this was a white-knuckle flight from start to finish. Smoke and flames belched out of the prop engine on my side of the plane. The bolts that fastened my seat to the floor were either loose or broken. I could actually lift the seat up from the floor a few inches. I also noticed that parts of the plane's interior wall had pulled away. When the air conditioning came on, I thought for a moment we were being gassed. White smoke rolled down from the ceiling like the vapors from a large cube of dry ice. I figured that with my luck the plane would go down and crash in a minefield, killing me twice. Yet somehow this wreck made it to Tan Son Nhut. It was the first time I had seen my old home in 27 years.

And that was all I would see. Our papers were not, after all, completely in order. Communist authorities refused to let us leave the airport. Mark was traveling as a private citizen and not as a Foreign Service officer, so he couldn't pull any rank. After an hour or so, another communist functionary in an ill-fitting dark green uniform told us that we were being deported. They locked us into what we called the First-Class Deportation Lounge and told us to wait there for the next available flight back to Phnom Penh. So there we waited four or five hours. I could see across the runway to where I had once worked at the Research & Analysis Branch. I wondered how the old building was being used. Finally, when our flight arrived, we were marched to the boarding ramp. After so many years of waiting, it was a disappointment not to be able to poke around more.

Once back in Phnom Penh, we tried again to gain permission to enter Vietnam. We got all the right stamps and signatures. Again we flew to Saigon—this time on a Vietnam Airline plane, which I took as a hopeful sign. The apparatchiks at the airport let us go and we grabbed a cab for downtown. The driver turned out

Henry Billings

to be a former major in the South Vietnamese military who had spent ten years in a reeducation camp. I asked him about the old Saigon Golf Club. He said the communist leadership had converted the golf course into a housing project. (Maybe I should have supported the war, after all.)

Mark and I spent that night at the Rex Hotel. There was a rotary circle in front of the hotel. In the middle of the rotary was a small garden and pool. Back in the days of what the Vietnamese now call "the American war," there was also a huge billboard in the middle of the garden. It had the flags of two dozen nations that supported, in one form or another, the South Vietnamese government. On the billboard was a message written in English which read in part, "Long live the spirit of mutual assistance of the peoples and governments of the Free World Nations. The Vietnamese people are grateful for the assistance of friendly nations. Every measure of assistance is a new step towards the triumph of freedom over slavery." I wondered what the communists had done with that billboard.

All the old go-go bars in the city were gone. But Saigon had a few new bars to take their place. The most famous was the Apocalypse Now Bar. It featured black walls, loud music and the blade of a real helicopter suspended from the ceiling. When the rock music wasn't playing, they pumped in the thump, thump sound of a helicopter blade. Most of the customers were Westerners, some were American ex-pats. (The bar has since been moved to a larger building and has become a must-see tourist trap.)

*****

In the end, my 1993 experience in Vietnam was a disappointment. I had hoped to see more. I had hoped to spend more time walking around Saigon. But I had gotten a little taste and wanted more. Then, in 2001, I finally went back again and did it right. This time I went for three full weeks, which included

VIETNAM FOLLIES
A Memoir of an Intelligence Officer

the Tet (Vietnamese New Year) holiday, on a combination sea kayaking and bike tour organized by VeloAsia, an American tour company. The trip began in Hanoi, the shrine to Ho Chi Minh disguised as a city. Everywhere I looked were reminders of Uncle Ho's achievements. There was Ho Chi Minh's Mausoleum, a not-so-subtle Soviet-built marble structure in the center of town. There was the Ho Chi Minh Museum, which presented Ho's life story, his cane, his bed, his pith helmet, his car, his loom, drafts of his speeches, and lots of photos. Behind the mausoleum was the house where he had lived and worked from 1958 until his death in 1969. The house was built on stilts next to a small lake. Our tour guide, a intelligent young woman named Diep, spoke of Uncle Ho in reverential, almost mystical, tones. She referred to Ho Chi Minh, who had no children, as the father of 73 million Vietnamese. To hear her talk, Ho also planted every tree in Hanoi, stocked every fish pond, and probably carved every statue of himself found all over the country. I had to remind myself than I was in Hanoi and not in Graceland.

Clearly, to the North Vietnamese at least, Ho Chi Minh remained a combination of Jesus Christ and George Washington. This was driven home to me during a visit to the Old Quarter of Hanoi. The Old Quarter is a confusing maze of narrow streets and alleyways lined with specialty shops and food stalls. Diep led us into a narrow alleyway that opened into a series of small rooms on one side. Each room served as home for a Vietnamese family. The rooms had no windows and the only light came from a fluorescent lamp or two. Diep led us into a home where she offered an elderly couple a gift for Tet. The couple offered the six of us tourists a place to sit while they stood. The 82-year-old man's proudest possession, which he insisted we study closely, was a photograph of him with a waving and smiling Ho Chi Minh taken in 1956. In the photo, the man is part of a group of at least 100 soldiers. Ho stands at least 20 feet away from him. Yet this fleeting encounter with Ho Chi Minh still brought a broad smile to the old man's face.

The contrast between Hanoi and Saigon can hardly be exaggerated. In fact, Hanoi and Saigon didn't seem to be part of the same country. The differences were striking, and they cut across cultural, economic, and philosophical lines. In Saigon, for example, I saw communist flags here and there but nowhere near the number I saw in Hanoi. In Hanoi, many people still wear those dark green army sun helmets that Jane Fonda made famous when she donned one during her notorious wartime visit to the city. In Saigon, no one wears that helmet. Hanoi still has the smell of an old, decaying city. Saigon has the feel of a modern metropolis.

Also, there is still much bitterness in Saigon over the treatment the South Vietnamese received from their masters in the North. First there were the reeducation camps. Then there was the confiscation of personal wealth. (Southerners had to trade in 10 old dong to get one new dong. Northerners got to trade one old dong for one new dong. Later, the exchange rate dropped to 5 for 1 in the South but the Northerners continued to trade at par.) And, for a long time, Southerners were denied any important leadership roles in their own government. (The real losers in the Vietnam War were not the Americans but the Viet Cong. They suffered hideous casualties yet lost control of their own revolution to the North Vietnamese after 1975.)

Le Van Sinh, our guide in the South, told me he has learned to live with the communists. But it hasn't been easy. Ten times in the late 1970's and 1980's his family paid money to help him flee the country by boat. Each time the communist patrol boats stopped him and he had to swim to shore to avoid capture. His family stopped trying only when they ran out of money. Even now when Sinh inadvertently uses pet communist phrases such as "solidarity" or "reunification," his father scolds him for talking like a communist.

VIETNAM FOLLIES
A Memoir of an Intelligence Officer

Now, at the beginning of the 21st century, most of the central planning blunders of the early years of communist rule have been reversed. The leaders have dropped their insistence on the collective agriculture that nearly starved the nation. Under that system, people had to line up each month to receive the most meager of rations. Tran Thanh Hai, our guide to Ha Long Bay and Hanoi, said he had spent hours each day waiting in one line or another for a cup of sugar or a few ounces of rice. (Hai didn't let the system crush his spirit, however. He used his free time to study English by reading the banned *Animal Farm* and *1984* with phony glued-on covers.) Communist leaders have also recognized the need to reward individual workers for their efforts. Hai told us that the state used to pay all pottery workers a common monthly wage. But with everyone getting identical pay, there was no incentive to work hard. Eventually, the communists recognized their folly and introduced a capitalist wage system—piecework. Production boomed.

Vietnam's economic turnaround began in 1986 when the Vietnamese, following the lead set by the Soviets, opened up their economy. The new official slogan was "to change or to die." Tens of thousands of enterprising Vietnamese went into business for themselves. Highway One, which runs between Hanoi and Saigon, is lined with small shops and roadside stands. It seems all a person needs to open a business along this road is a dozen bottles of orange Fanta, a few packs of chewing gum, and some one-liter bottles filled with gasoline for motorbikes. As Hai told me, to most Vietnamese "it is better to be the head of a chicken than the tail of an elephant."

By the time of my 2001 trip, there were very few signs that Vietnam was a communist-ruled nation. True, there were many large billboards showing "socialist art." Often they featured proud farmers, factory workers, or students with ruby-red lips gazing off into the distance in blissful contemplation of their bright future. But this was not like visiting Russia or any eastern European nation when they were under Soviet control. There

Henry Billings

were no restrictions on where we could go or who could talk to us. Also, the people were not afraid to be critical of their government. We couldn't take photographs of military bases, but that seemed fair enough and in such a beautiful country no one in our group was interested in the military anyway. The only other sign of communism was the outrageous featherbedding at the toll booths on the road from Hanoi to Haiphong. Each small booth had three people. One person collected tolls on the traffic heading east, one collecting tolls on west-bound traffic, and the third supervised the first two.

*****

The problems of Vietnam and how the Vietnamese choose to solve them is not, and never has been, my business. This attitude left me distinctly in the minority back in 1965. The United States decided to make Vietnamese affairs our affairs and the evidence of that interference can still be seen. On the road from Hanoi to Haiphong, I could still see damage to bridges and bomb craters in fields. The ever-resourceful Vietnamese have turned the bomb craters into fish ponds. They also use empty bomb shells as village bells and transform explosives from duds into fireworks. Everyone on our bike tour was struck by just how desperately poor these people remain and we all wondered why in God's name we once thought it was a good thing to bomb the crap out of these people.

War museums in Hanoi and Saigon – sooner or later every war becomes a tourist attraction—offer stark and graphically one-sided testimony of the inhumanity of modern war as practiced by the French and the Americans. (The communists were brutal, too, but no mention is made of that.) The museums are pretty sobering places to visit. The War Remnants Museum, once called the Museum of American War Crimes, is particularly grim, with its photos showing victims of napalm and white phosphorous bombs. I steeled myself for these museums and they didn't upset me in the way they might affect some people. I had seen similar photos before.

The My Lai Memorial was the worst of all. It easily trumped all the others. This place, about eight miles from Quang Ngai, was where 504 people were murdered in cold blood by Americans. In the small museum building, I gazed at an exhibit of some burnt household utensils. As I did so, an elderly Vietnamese man came up to me and took my hand in friendship. He held it for a minute or so without saying a word. Then he squeezed my forearm and walked away.

Later, I toured each of the homes that were destroyed that terrible day of March 16, 1968. I placed an incense stick at each site. Simple plaques at each site gave the names and ages of the victims. Many were children or infants. I made the mistake of taking out pictures of my own children and pondering the cruelties of blind fate. Then I began to cry.

My Lai made me ashamed that I didn't do more to protest the war. Sending my medals back to the White House with an angry note wasn't enough. Neither was refusing to pay a tax or two because the money was used to support the war. Neither was penning an occasional letter to the editor or teaching my high school students about the war or going to a few anti-war protests. It wasn't enough, not nearly enough. I knew better and should have aimed higher. My Lai showed me that perhaps I didn't emerge from the Vietnam war unscathed. Perhaps the war did leave its scar on me after all.

Henry Billings

About the Author

After leaving the army in 1967, Henry Billings taught high school social studies for sixteen years. Along the way, he also began building a career as a freelance writer. Then, in 1984, he left teaching to become a full-time writer. A member of the American Society of Journalists and Authors for nearly two decades, he has written numerous newspaper and magazines articles. In addition, he has written two non-fiction trade books as well as more than 100 books for the school market. His works have been published by McGraw-Hill, Jamestown, New England Press, EMC Publishing, Young People's Press, People's Publishing Group, and Children's Press.